Praise for INCENTIVES FOR CHANGE . . .

"Truly inspirational for parents looking to find ways to motivate their children with autism."

—Vincent Spinelli, parent and board member,
The New Jersey Center for Outreach Services
for the Autism Community (COSAC)

"To help individuals with autism spectrum disorders, parents and professionals need to know how to motivate them to learn new skills and use ones they already have. This easy-to-read yet sophisticated book helps to meet this crucial challenge. The book abounds with up-to-date information, useful tips, and realistic case examples of individuals with autism spectrum disorders at many different ages and skill levels. A valuable resource for both new and experienced caregivers. Highly recommended!"

—Tristram Smith, Ph.D., Assistant Professor of Pediatrics (Psychology),
Strong Center for Developmental Disabilities,
University of Rochester Medical Center

Topics in Autism

Incentives for Change

Motivating People with Autism Spectrum Disorders to Learn and Gain Independence

Lara Delmolino, Ph.D. &
Sandra L. Harris, Ph.D.

Sandra L. Harris, Ph.D., *series editor*

Woodbine House ◆ 2004

Published in the United States of America by Woodbine House, Inc., 6510 Bells
Mill Rd., Bethesda, MD 20817. 800-843-7323. www.woodbinehouse.com

Library of Congress Cataloging-in-Publication Data

Harris, Sandra L.
  Incentives for change : motivating people with autism spectrum disorders to
learn and gain independence / Sandra L. Harris and Lara Delmolino.-- 1st ed.
      p. cm. — (Topics in autism)
  Includes bibliographical references and index.
  ISBN 1-890627-60-7
  1. Autistic children. 2. Motivation (Psychology) in children. I. Delmolino, Lara.
II. Title. III. Series.

RJ506.A9H2687 2004
649'.154—dc22

                                                                    2004019940

Manufactured in the United States of America

First edition

10 9 8 7 6 5 4 3 2 1

For Leonard and Bette Delmolino,
with gratitude for years of love and support

And for Rhona Leibel,
who has brought Sandra
a lifetime of friendship and wisdom

TABLE OF CONTENTS

Preface ix

Chapter 1   Motivating the Child with Autism:
An Introduction 1

Chapter 2   Identifying the Reinforcers: "I Like That" 19

Chapter 3   Mand Training: "Give Me That" 47

Chapter 4   Making Choices: "I Prefer That" 73

Chapter 5   Token Systems: "I'll Buy That" 95

Chapter 6   Self-Management: "I Can Do It Myself" 121

Index 141

PREFACE

Respecting the individuality of children or students with autism spectrum disorders requires ongoing sensitive observation on our part as parents or teachers. We want to know enough about each learner to create an environment that will maximize his or her motivation to learn, as well as support a sense of personal autonomy. Finding the right incentives to support the learning of children, adolescents, and adults with autism is one of the first crucial steps in teaching them new skills.

Identifying potential reinforcers is easy for some individuals with autism spectrum disorders. They love certain foods, toys, music, etc., and would climb any mountain to gain access to those items. For these students, it is often easy to move an instructional program into high gear. For many other children, however, the process is more daunting. They may be willing to work for one or two items, but once they have had enough of that item (e.g., juice) it is hard to find something else to attract their attention. In addition, a smaller number of individuals on the autism spectrum seem indifferent to our early efforts to offer *any* kind of potential incentive for even a small bit of work. Working with these youngsters is initially much more daunting than working with easier-to-motivate students.

As authors, the two of us share nearly a half-century of work with people with autism. That includes children, adolescents, and adults across the autism spectrum and with varying degrees of mental retardation. Over the years, we have worked closely both with learners who were easy to motivate, and with those who were more difficult. The good news from our perspective is that there are an increasing number of well-developed tools for creating motivational systems for students with autism. Descriptions of these tools are found in a variety of different professional sources and are discussed in different contexts. We do not, however, know of one source that summarizes for the interested parent or teacher the range of potential incentive systems that can be used. Given the universal need for some sort of incentive system for every learner—from the youngest to the oldest, and from the most to least receptive—we thought it would be helpful to pull this information together in one place. That is what we have attempted to do in this book.

The kinds of incentive systems we describe cover a full range of needs. That includes identifying simple reinforcers for young learners who need an immediate tangible reward as well as delayed reinforcements for older students who can wait a while and work toward a bigger goal. We describe formal and informal ways to identify potential reinforcers, how to assess a child's current motivation, and, at the more advanced level, how to teach an individual to manage his or her own incentive system. Some chapters may be immediately useful for your child, and other material may not apply now, but will be goals for you to work toward.

The material in this book can be helpful for people with autism of any age and specific diagnosis, including Autistic Disorder, Asperger's Disorder, PDD-NOS, or Childhood Disintegrative Disorder. Although some chapters are more clearly aimed at very young children who are first learning to initiate interactions and follow simple directions, that does not mean that an older student who never had such training cannot benefit from the same programs. Draw from these pages what is right for your child or student.

We are both grateful for the on-going support of our colleagues at the Douglass Developmental Disabilities Center, including Maria Arnold, Marlene Brown, Marlene Cohen, Rita Gordon, Jan Handleman, Barbara Kristoff, Robert LaRue, Donna Sloan, Mary Jane Weiss, and Jackie Wright. We thank also the several generations of parents and children who have taught us about autism. We are indebted to these families for the trust they placed in us and in the Douglass Developmental Disabilities Center. We hope they will take pride in knowing that what they taught us has become part of this book.

We appreciate the willingness of the following families to contribute the photos that brighten our pages: Cathy and Tom Avasso (Michael), Marlene and Marty Cohen (Chelsea), Ilona Harris & Gary Zuckerman (Emma & Molly), Joelle Lugo and Joe Testa (Enzo), and Beth and Greg Troiano (Emma).

Lara thanks Chris for his love, support, and companionship, and Brooke, for bringing new meaning to their life together. She also expresses gratitude to her grandmother, Mary Liley, for her strength, wisdom, and inspiration. Lastly, she appreciates the joy brought to her life by Peter, Francesca, Emma, and Anthony.

Sandra owes special thanks to Joseph Masling, who, as her graduate school mentor, taught her how to be a scientist-practitioner, and to Jean Burton, her faculty mentor, who helped her become a pretty good teacher. She also thanks her brother Jay for a lifetime of brotherly love, and Ilona, Gary, Emma, Molly, and Jake, who bring their love into her life.

Rutgers, The State University
Fall, 2004

1 | Motivating the Child with Autism: An Introduction

The Barton Family

Maddy and Mitch Barton have two children. Their eldest, nine-year-old Sarah, is an enthusiastic, intense girl who is always quick to please and who is passionate about soccer, rock climbing, ballet, and reading. What delights her and what matters to her are easy for her parents to discern. Their younger child, Charlie, is another story. Charlie, who is nearly four, has autism. He has been enrolled in a preschool program for children with autism for the past two months and has made some progress, but is still a handful at home and often at school as well. One of the big challenges everyone faces is trying to figure out what matters to Charlie. Nothing seems to excite or delight him very much, and he appears to prefer flapping his hands to eating ice cream or playing with his toys. Unlike his sister, Charlie does not appear very interested in his parents' praise and affection, nor do their frowns or firm "no's" have much influence on his behavior. For the Bartons, Charlie is in many respects a puzzle.

During a home visit by Charlie's teacher, Caroline Saunders, the Bartons shared their problems in motivating Charlie to do the things he needs to do. Caroline, who had been working with Charlie in the classroom for several weeks, said that she could understand the Bartons' concerns because she too was having trouble finding ways to motivate him. She said that she was going to do some very systematic evaluations of the things that seemed to matter to Charlie. She then planned to use that information to try to make school an appealing place where Charlie could work for things he wanted. She hoped to collaborate with the Bartons to help them identify ways to motivate Charlie at home as well.

The first step Caroline suggested to Maddy and Mitch was to regularly observe how Charlie spends his time when no one is making any demands on him. Are there objects he seeks out? Places he prefers to go? Foods that interest him? Videos he wants to watch? She asked them to make these observations several times each day, taking notes on what attracted Charlie's interest, and how long he pursued a particular activity. Caroline was going to do the same thing at school and see if she could find any clear preferences in that setting. If nothing emerged from this very simple assessment, she said there were more elaborate methods they could use to try to tap in to the things that might interest Charlie. In addition, she would ask the school psychologist for a consultation, if need be.

Discussion

The challenge facing Charlie's parents and teacher is not an unusual one for adults who care about children on the autism spectrum. Although some youngsters with autism may have clear-cut preferences for particular items or activities, for others it is much harder to identify the things that delight them. Even among children who do seem to enjoy specific foods or toys, it is important to ensure that there is a broad range of potential motivators available so that we can shift the incentives as the child's interests change. Most people, including children on the autism spectrum, have a limit to how many graham crackers, tickles, or minutes on a swing they enjoy before the pleasure fades and they seek other forms of stimulation.

If we are to support the learning of a child with autism, ideally we should have a range of rewards we can offer for the effort they must put forth to learn. Sometimes identifying these motivating factors is relatively easy, but for some children such as Charlie, it requires systemic efforts on the part of parents and teachers to determine what will motivate the child with autism to work toward a learning goal.

What Is Different about Children on the Autism Spectrum?

Why doesn't Charlie enjoy his parents' attention and the many attractive toys they have gotten for him? Why won't he do even simple things such as clap his hands just to please them? People who are not familiar with the impact of autism are often baffled by how difficult it can be to motivate these students to do even simple tasks. They wonder if the child is being willful and difficult, or if he is simply not capable of complying with what appear to

be easy requests. As one becomes familiar with the impact of autism on how a child learns, it becomes evident that multiple factors may be involved in this issue of "motivation."

Most infants appear biologically predisposed to enjoy the cuddles, hugs, and tickles their parents provide, just as most parents revel in this contact with their babies. These physically pleasurable experiences are often accompanied by words of endearment, and these words gradually take on a great deal of inherent pleasure for the baby from being associated with the physically pleasant sensations of being cuddled. When a baby hears the words, "Here is my little love," and his father then picks him up and snuggles him, he gradually builds an association between the pleasure of his father's arms and the words his father utters as he picks him up.

Most children learn very early that doing things that please their parents brings them liberal doses of affection, whereas less desirable behaviors may be ignored or corrected with a mild reprimand such as "no" or "stop." Their parents' praise and affection become powerful sources of motivation for most typically developing children whose parents provide them with even a modest level of attention. You don't have to be a certified teacher or a psychologist to give this experience to a baby; most adults can do a pretty good job of nurturing. From such early beginnings grow our motivation to please other people and do the right thing.

This motivation to please is important both for all the lessons that parents must teach their children about safety, appropriate social behavior, and so forth, and for when children get to school. Although some school lessons may be inherently interesting to a child and some classroom activities delightful, school is also filled with demands that may not appeal to a child. Children learn to sit in a circle, raise their hands, and share materials—not necessarily because these are fun things to do, but because adults expect them to comply and because pleasing adults is important to most children. Certainly for most children, learning new knowledge and skills is engaging, and being at school carries considerable reinforcement value. However, for most of us, the pleasure of learning alone is not sufficient to carry us through the rigor of learning.

Unlike the typically developing child, the youngster with autism may not find his parent's praise, smiles, and hugs very powerful in motivating him to work hard. These children have a problem learning the links between their behavior and their parents' responses. Deficits in social learning make their understanding of the world very confusing and difficult to organize. In addition, some children have mental retardation along with autism and find it very difficult to understand the tasks they are being asked to do. For them there is a double challenge of simply comprehending what they are supposed to do and of being motivated to work for the approval and praise of their parents. Even very bright children on the autism spectrum may not find praise or physical affection a very powerful incentive to do the exceptionally hard work they must do to learn, or they may not link their parent's behavior to the task they are expected to perform. The world of the young child with autism is a bewildering place.

Because many of the things we ask children with autism to do are very challenging for them to master, they often learn to avoid or escape our requests with behaviors that can range from slipping to the floor to having a full-fledged tantrum to hitting the teacher. These are not the responses of a "bad" or defiant child, but rather ones that he has learned will get him out of difficult learning situations or will keep him from having to stop an enjoyable activity. For some children, flipping their fingers in front of their eyes, rocking back and forth, or lining up toy cars is much more gratifying than answering a parent's question or pointing to an object on request. These initial preferences are inherent in the nature of autism. It is our role as parents or teachers to help the child learn to value other activities that *we* view as important and the purpose of this book to suggest a variety of ways to accomplish that kind of change in motivation. Once we find effective ways to motivate children with autism as learners and give them ways to communicate their need for help with tasks, many of these escape or avoidance behaviors will diminish.

In addition to not finding other people's praise and approval motivating, children on the autism spectrum have other learning problems. One of these is their decreased interest in imitating what other people do. Very young typically developing babies will imitate some of the facial expressions of adults and are very attuned to what adults do. For example, when six-month-old Alexandra's father leans over her crib and makes popping sounds with his lips, she will respond by smacking her own lips. As children get older, they enjoy doing things "just like a grown up." At eighteen months of age, Jack will take his parents' keys and attempt to unlock the door. This imitation grows more complex with age and is incorporated into children's play as they pretend to cook a meal and take pride in serving it to their parents, pretend to shave just as Daddy does in the morning, or put their baby doll down for a nap just as Mommy does for them.

For typically developing children, the process of pretending is inherently reinforcing and motivating. By contrast, pretend play is very difficult for children with autism to master and rarely emerges with the rich complexity of their typically developing peers. The lack of intrinsic reinforcement that is available from social imitation and more elaborate pretend play cuts off another avenue of learning and motivation for the child with autism. Although this book does not address teaching social and play skills, another book in this series, *Reaching Out, Joining In* (Weiss & Harris, 2001), discusses teaching these skills at some length. What you will learn in the present book is how to motivate your child to learn those social lessons.

One other topic we will not address in any detail is reducing maladaptive behavior such as stereotyped movements, self-injury, or aggression. These are important questions, but beyond the scope of this book, since an entire, complex set of skills is required to deal with them. If your child does engage in significant maladaptive behavior, you will want to consult with a Board Certified Behavior Analyst or your child's teacher about how to assess the behavior and identify the factors that are reinforcing it and maintaining it over time. Based on that information, you can develop an intervention plan to teach your child alternatives to the inappropriate behavior. Your skills at using reinforcement will become very important at that stage. For a very brief discussion of reduction of maladaptive behavior in one of our adult clients see Chapter 4. The process of treating seriously maladaptive behavior is itself worthy of entire books. Two you might look at are *Functional Assessment and Program Development for Problem Behavior* (O'Neill et al., 1990) and *Behavior Modification* (Miltenberger, 2001).

What Is Applied Behavior Analysis?

The learning problems of children with autism have responded well to the teaching methods of Applied Behavior Analysis (ABA). Because of its documented benefits in educating these youngsters, we use the methods of ABA in our own work and will share them with you in this book. Applied Behavior Analysis is a scientific approach to understanding how people learn. The people who use these methods, Applied Behavior Analysts, place a high value on using methods that bring about socially meaningful changes in behavior. We make the personal welfare of the individual the heart of our teaching because we believe that the changes we bring about should be big enough and important enough to have a meaningful impact on the quality of a person's life. We also try to be very efficient in bringing about those changes and to draw our teaching methods from the research literature, because we want to use methods that have been shown to be effective. There is considerable research in the field of ABA and it helps us to separate what is likely to work well from what has not been found useful.

We will present some of the important principles of ABA in this book and discuss them in some depth. If you want to learn more about ABA, there are some helpful introductory books, including one of our own books, *Right from the Start: Behavioral Intervention for Young Children with Autism* (Harris & Weiss, 1998), and a book edited by Catherine Maurice and her colleagues, *Making a Difference* (2001). If you want a very sophisticated, advanced text in this area, try *Applied Behavior Analysis* (Cooper, Heron & Heward, 1987).

What Is Reinforcement?

To be effective at using ABA methods to teach your child, one of the key ABA concepts you need to understand is that of reinforcement, or, as it is sometimes called informally, reward. We have already used the term *reward* a number of times in this first chapter and it is important to offer you a preliminary, working definition of what we mean when we say *reinforcement*. Later we will examine the concept in greater detail.

Positive Reinforcement

You will read a great deal in this book about using positive reinforcement to increase desirable behavior. People who use the principles of Applied Behavior Analysis to educate children with autism rely heavily on positive reinforcement to help children learn.

In Applied Behavior Analysis, the term *positive reinforcement* has a very specific and technical definition, which may differ from how people generally think about positive reinforcement in everyday language. From an Applied Behavior Analysis perspective, positive reinforcement refers to any event or environmental change that increases the likelihood that an individual will repeat a behavior that occurred just before the reinforcement. For example, if we wanted a child to touch his head, we could present him with a bit of ice cream each time he followed the direction, "Touch your head." If that resulted in his touching his head more often, we would know the ice cream had functioned as a positive reinforcement.

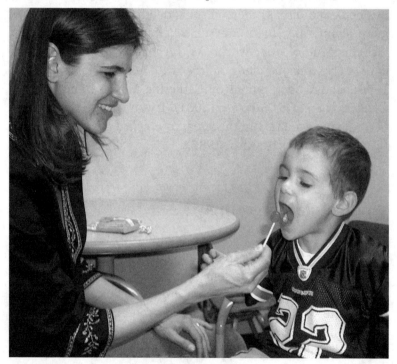

It is important to make no assumptions about whether a specific event is positively reinforcing. Not everyone enjoys candy, tickles, watching television, or having a backrub. Some people do and some people don't. Some children with autism may learn quickly when offered pieces of cookie, spoons of ice cream, tummy rubs, or time to play with a favorite car, while others will ignore these items. When it comes to positive reinforcement, one person's "meat" is another person's "poison."

The key point to remember is that an item or event can only be defined as positive reinforcement if we measure its effect on behavior and determine that behavior increases when the item is provided following a particular behavior. For example, say you noticed that your typically developing daughter was not doing any reading during the summer, so you offered her $2.00 for every book she completed and wrote a short report on. You would know the money was a positive reinforcement if she then read more books than she had before. Similarly, if your child on the autism spectrum almost never comes when you call his name and you decide that you will toss him in the air each time he does come, you will know the tossing is a positive reinforcement if he now comes more often. If you see no change in how often he comes, you have to think about a different way to motivate him.

Some people ask whether giving a child a reinforcer for doing what "he ought to do" is a form of bribery. They believe that a child should want to do the right thing. For many of us, knowing that we are "doing the right thing" can in fact be very motivating. It leads soldiers to take great risks on behalf of their comrades and their country, and is the reason parents get up in the middle of the night to care for a crying child. As we mature, the positive reinforcement that created these caring values becomes more and more subtle to detect by an outsider because the reinforcement mostly involves what we say to ourselves. In contrast, when a young child shares a cookie with his sister, the praise he receives from his father may be a big part of what makes the sharing likely to be repeated. So, when we consider what we "ought" to do, it is important to ask what the expectations are for people at different stages in their lives and how people learn these appropriate behaviors to begin with.

Considering positive reinforcement as "bribery" is also misleading because society uses the word bribery to imply that we are being rewarded for doing something that is wrong. Bribery is used to persuade a person to give false testimony, provide insider trading information, and so forth. People go to prison for bribery. Such conduct is radically different from finding some desirable incentive to increase the effort of a child with autism to learn the many difficult lessons he must master. Giving those incentives is no more bribery than is giving an employee a paycheck every week that he works, or telling a student that he will graduate with special honors if he earns the highest average in his school.

Negative Reinforcement

Another ABA term that is useful to know is *negative reinforcement*. Contrary to common belief, this does not mean punishing a person. Rather, negative reinforcement refers to ending an undesirable event. For example, when Tom's parents put certain vegetables in front of him, he pushes them off the table. They introduced a program to teach Tom to say, "No, thank you" when offered one of these vegetables, and if he does say "No, thank you," the vegetable is removed. Saying "No, thank you" is negatively reinforced because it results in the removal of the unwanted food. We will not discuss the use of negative reinforcement in any detail in this book because it is more complex to use and not as central to good teaching as is positive reinforcement. If you want more information, ask a Board Certified Behavior Analyst or see the discussion of the term in the book by Cooper et al. (1987) or another introduction to ABA.

For the sake of brevity, we will most often use the term *reinforcement* or *reinforcer* without the modifier of *positive* or *negative*. Unless we call an event negative reinforcement, you should assume we are talking about positive reinforcement.

Points to Remember

The two important points to remember about a reinforcer, either positive or negative, are that:

1. it is an item or event that is delivered after a person has engaged in a behavior, that
2. results in an increase in the occurrence of that behavior.

Note that a reinforcer is given after the behavior, not before, and that there must be an increase in the behavior for the item or event to be considered a reinforcer.

Table 1-1 | Reinforcement

- ◆ Give after the desired behavior
- ◆ Give quickly
- ◆ Only reinforcing if behavior increases
- ◆ Be enthusiastic
- ◆ Link tangible rewards with social reinforcers
- ◆ More creative/novel responses get more reinforcement
- ◆ Vary reinforcers

How Do You Deliver Reinforcement?

Decades of research on the use of reinforcement with children on the autism spectrum as well as their typically developing peers have shown that there are some fundamental rules to follow in using this teaching tool effectively and efficiently.

Give It Immediately

It is important to give reinforcement immediately after the behavior you wish to increase. If you wait for even a few seconds, another behavior may pop up and you will find yourself reinforcing something that you do not wish to increase. For example, if you ask your child to "Touch blue" and he does so, but then waves his fingers in front of his face before you can offer him a bit of ice cream, you may risk rewarding stereotypic finger waving rather than touching blue. This kind of mistake makes teaching less efficient and should be avoided whenever possible. However, we all make some errors when we teach, and, as long as you do not routinely reinforce an undesirable behavior, you are not likely to make it much worse if you make an occasional slip.

To avoid reinforcing the wrong behavior, have your reinforcing item close at hand and offer it before you do anything else. If your child does manage to slip in an inappropriate behavior, do not provide reinforcement, but go on to the next trial or make another request.

Vary Reinforcers

It is also important to vary the items you use as reinforcers. If your child likes juice and you give him many sips of juice, at some point he will be satiated and lose interest in the juice. You might alternate juice and pretzels to maintain his interest in juice, or you might offer a very different reinforcement such as fifteen seconds of a favorite video or some tickles. For most of us, variety is the spice of life. Chapter 2 explains how to identify an array of objects and events that are reinforcing to your child.

Link Tangible Reinforcers with Intangible Reinforcers

Another essential guideline is to link tangible reinforcers such as juice, cookies, or toys with your own loving behavior toward your child. Although some children with autism may not initially value praise and smiles, these should be consistently paired with things that are reinforcing. Over time, these social reinforcers will become more rewarding to your child, and you will be able to decrease the use of more tangible reinforcements.

The technical name for presenting an established reinforcer with an event that you wish to make into a reinforcer is "pairing." For example, you can pair a sip of juice (which is already reinforcing) with praise (which you want to establish as a reinforcer). To do this, you would say "Great work," as you hand the child his cup of juice. By doing this many, many times, the praise will gradually take on the same reinforcing power as the juice. The established reinforcer does not have to be something tangible such as food or a toy. You could pair praise with a token in order to make the token something with immediate reinforcement value. In Chapter 5, we describe how to make tokens reinforcing for children with autism.

Make the Effort Match the Outcome

It is also a good idea to match the quality of the reinforcement to the quality of the response. Initially, you will reinforce every effort your child makes to respond, but gradually you will raise your standard. For example, if your child knows how to say "cup" clearly and makes only a half-hearted effort to say it, you might give only a small reinforcement such as, "Right, it is a cup," and then give a much more significant reinforcement when he makes a better response. A creative or much improved response such as saying, "Cup juice" for the first time is a good opportunity to bring out the brass band! Make novel or creative responses the occasion for a great deal of enthusiasm.

What Is Reinforcing?

In Chapter 2 we will discuss in depth how to identify reinforcers for your child and how to create new reinforcements by linking new items with ones that are already reinforcing. We also discuss how to identify reinforcements for the hard-to-motivate child. Our purpose in this chapter is just to introduce the concept.

Table 1-2 | Some Reinforcing Items and Experiences

Edibles
- Cereal
- Yogurt
- Ice cream
- Pickles
- Olives
- Jam
- Cookies
- Crackers
- Juice
- Soda
- Water

Interactions
- Being tossed in the air
- Tickles
- Hugs
- Massage
- Peek-a-Boo

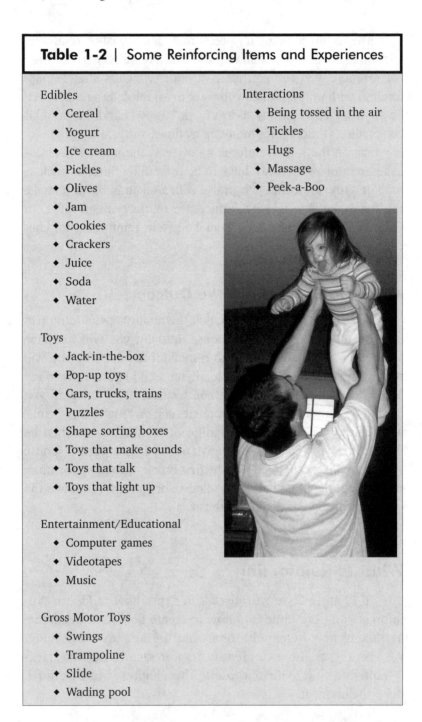

Toys
- Jack-in-the-box
- Pop-up toys
- Cars, trucks, trains
- Puzzles
- Shape sorting boxes
- Toys that make sounds
- Toys that talk
- Toys that light up

Entertainment/Educational
- Computer games
- Videotapes
- Music

Gross Motor Toys
- Swings
- Trampoline
- Slide
- Wading pool

As Table 1-2 indicates, many items are potentially reinforcing for a child. That includes a broad range of food, from tiny candies to olives and pickles or yogurt. What works is, of course, distinctive to each of us. Some of us like dill pickles, some like sweet and sour, and some people you could chase with a pickle! It is also useful and important to think beyond food and consider the broad array of other experiences that are potentially motivating for a child. That can include favorite toys, videos, games, running, jumping, being tossed in the air, and so forth. For many children, cuddles, tickles, and hugs may have reinforcing value or may gradually acquire that power by being paired with other events that are already reinforcing. Similarly, words of praise may not mean much to your child now, but may become very powerful if they are consistently paired with other items that are already motivating.

Although some parents may worry that giving too many food reinforcers may cause a child to become overweight, we have not seen that as an issue among our students. First, the size of each reward is small. Second, when we use food, we try to offer a range of foods the child enjoys, not just sweet or fatty foods. Finally, food is a starting point, not an end goal, and we wean a child from food to other incentives as soon as we can.

It is very helpful if a child can learn to ask for the things he wants. Chapter 3 will introduce you to the concept of "Mand Training" as a way to teach a child to initiate requests for desired items. Once your child can make these requests, you no longer have to guess so much about what will be motivating. Being able to "mand" is very powerful for a child because it helps him achieve his goals and because it is an interpersonal behavior in which he asks another person for the items he wants.

From Today to the Future: Food to Self-Sufficiency

Although food, tickles, and hugs may be high on your child's current list of preferences for reinforcers, ultimately you want him to be motivated by his own feelings of achievement, by a paycheck, or by other reinforcement that he can give himself. This book is not limited to discussing the use of tangible reinforcers that appeal to a young child, but also considers how to move a child toward appreciating more abstract reinforcement. For example, Chapter 5 addresses the use of token systems, where pennies, poker chips, or other small symbolic rewards are exchanged for items that the individual wishes to "buy," such as time watching television, bags of potato chips, or weekend trips.

We also want learners to be able to make choices both among work tasks and among different reinforcing items and Chapter 4 describes how to teach a child to make these choices. For example, a child might be taught how to arrange photographs of his activities in the order in which he wishes to do them or pick his reinforcer from an array of items.

Much of what we do as adults involves managing our own schedules, including reinforcing ourselves. We take a break after we finish cleaning the living room, count calories to lose weight, or save our money so we can buy an item that we really want. Delaying a break, saving money, and planning our day are all self-management skills. People with autism can learn these skills as well, and in Chapter 6, we will discuss methods of teaching self-management in more detail.

Summary

This book addresses ways to motivate children with autism to learn new behaviors and to control responses such as tantrums or aggression that may be interfering with their appropriate behavior. Motivation is central to learning, and, because the characteristics of autism interfere with learning, it is especially important to think carefully about how to help these youngsters be motivated to cooperate and learn. In order to develop an effective motivational system, it is important to understand the concept of reinforcement and how to identify and deliver items or events that are reinforcing for a child.

The chapters that follow will explore in detail important aspects of motivation. Chapter 2 is concerned with how to identify reinforcers for a child with an autism spectrum disorder, Chapter 3 focuses on teaching a person with autism ask for what he wants, Chapter 4 provides guidelines for supporting students in learning to make their own choices. In Chapter 5, we describe token systems, and in Chapter 6, we will consider ways to help more advanced students learn to manage their own behavior, including providing their own reinforcements. Note that we will use the term "autism" and "autism spectrum" interchangeably to refer to this broad category of people.

References

Cooper, J.O., Heron, T.E. & Heward, W. L. (1987). *Applied Behavior Analysis.* Upper Saddle River, NJ: Merrill.

Harris, S. L. & Weiss, M.J. (1998). *Right from the Start: Behavioral Intervention for Young Children with Autism.* Bethesda, MD: Woodbine House.

Maurice, C., Green, G. & Foxx, R.M. (Eds.) (2001). *Making a Difference.* Austin, TX: Pro-Ed.

Miltenberger, R. G. (2001). *Behavior Modification.* 2nd ed. Belmont, CA: Wadsworth.

O'Neill, R.E., Horner, R.H., Albin, R. W., Sprague, J. R., Storey, K. & Newton, J. S. (1997). *Functional Assessment and Program Development for Problem Behavior: A Practical Handbook.* Pacific Grove, CA: Brooks/Cole Publishing Co.

Weiss, M. J. & Harris, S.L. (2001). *Reaching Out, Joining In: Teaching Social Skills to Young Children with Autism.* Bethesda, MD: Woodbine House.

2 | Identifying Reinforcers: "I Like That"

The Brown Family

Ahmed and Lily Brown had been thrilled by the birth of their daughter, Maya. They had had problems conceiving a baby and were delighted when they finally succeeded. Maya was a beautiful, perfect looking little bundle who was very easy to care for as an infant. However, that picture changed between eighteen and twenty-four months as Maya gradually lost the few words she had learned and became increasingly difficult to manage. There were countless days when her parents were exhausted by the effort to find things that would interest her. She generally spurned their efforts to play with her, did not seem to enjoy the colorful toys that her young cousins offered her when they visited, and seemed indifferent when they came into her play space and took over the many appealing toys her parents provided. If Ahmed or Lily tried to entice Maya to do something by offering her a bit of food or a toy, she would typically just walk away, as if nothing seemed worth the effort.

Between twenty-four and thirty months, Maya became increasingly disinterested in her parents and her surroundings. She spent much of her time staring at her hands, rolling a rubber ball back and forth on the floor, and opening and closing the kitchen cabinet doors. She would shriek if any of the windows in the house were left open. Her diet consisted mainly of two different kinds of sugary cereal, soda, and olives. Some days even these few items had little appeal, and if her parents offered her one of them, she might turn away and ignore them.

The significance of these behaviors was not lost on Ahmed and Lily. Their nephew, Riley, now ten years old, had been diagnosed *with autism, and they saw the same behaviors in Maya that they had seen in Riley. As a result, they began to search for treatment options early. By the time Maya was thirty-six months old, she had been enrolled in an intensive, early intervention program for children with autism for several months. Maya had made some progress in the program, but the staff noted that there were few things that seemed to be effective as reinforcement. She had learned to ask for cereal and olives, but would work only briefly for these and then lose interest. Without a few more items of potential interest to Maya, it was difficult to engage her in learning for any extended period of time. Maya's teacher described to Ahmed and Lily her plans to do systematic work to identify items or experiences that Maya might find motivating.*

Discussion

It is not unusual for children with autism to find a relatively limited range of items reinforcing and it is often difficult for adults to anticipate what will be truly effective in motivating these young learners. The purpose of this chapter is to explain some very powerful concepts in applied behavior analysis: identifying *reinforcers* and understanding *establishing operations*. We will see how these concepts apply to children like Maya who are hard to motivate, as well as to children who are more accessible, but would benefit from having a broader range of potentially reinforcing items. We will first define the terms and then examine ways to identify potentially motivating items and experiences.

What Is Motivation?

People use the term *motivation* to refer to the reason why an individual does something. For instance, we might assume we know someone else's motivation and make comments along the lines of: She ate because she was hungry, he gossips because he likes to shock people, or he worked hard because he wanted to make something of himself. If we are to work effectively with children with autism, however, we will need a more precise understanding of motivation. It is not always as clear what is motivating for a child with autism as it might be for a typically developing child. To use the concept of motivation in our educational efforts we need to understand two concepts:

1. What is reinforcement? and
2. How does reinforcement motivate behavior?

What Is Reinforcement?

In Chapter 1 we discussed the definition and use of reinforcement at some length. We said there that reinforcement was something that happened after a person engaged in an activity and that increased the likelihood the person would do that behavior again. For example, if we give a child with autism a small spoonful of ice cream when she claps her hands, she will clap more often if ice cream is an effective reinforcer. If you want a more in-depth discussion of using reinforcement to motivate a child, see Chapter 1.

How Does Reinforcement Motivate Behavior?

This question is more complex. Why do we do the things we do? Certainly, there are activities for which the motivation seems to be part of the activity itself. For example, you may enjoy watching a movie, spending time with a friend, or eating a dish of ice cream. You see the same process in your typically developing children as they do things they seem to enjoy, such as watching a favorite video, playing with a particular toy, or eating a chocolate chip cookie warm out of the oven. In all these examples, there is motivation to engage in activities that bring pleasure.

Even when activities are inherently pleasurable, there are factors that naturally influence the extent of our motivation to engage in them. Eating that dish of ice cream may be less appealing after we have had a big meal. In the reverse, the ice cream may be especially appealing if we have been deprived of it for a long time. It is easy to see the changing motivation for items we consume, like food and drink. Sometimes we are full and sometimes we are hungry. This same principle applies to other activities. Spending time with a good friend may be less rewarding if you just spent a week traveling with her and would prefer some time alone. Likewise, we are all familiar with the phrase "Absence makes the heart grow fonder." We may be very motivated for our annual visit to see a good friend who lives far away.

These same factors, deprivation and satiation, influence the motivation of children. Chocolate chip cookies or candy will be even more appealing if a child can only have access to them on special occasions. Similarly, a child may be more motivated to watch her favorite video if she has not had an opportunity to watch it for a while. She may be more interested in attention from her mother after spending some time playing alone. This variation in the degree of motivation is natural. The intensity of motivation for items and activities naturally changes over time and is related to the availability of these pleasurable events.

There are other aspects to the concept of motivation that are important. What about activities that do not appear to be inherently pleasurable and motivating? Why do we get up when our alarm clock rings at 6 a.m., when the act of pulling ourselves from the bed does not bring us pleasure? It is likely that we may be motivated to avoid what would happen if we overslept. For example, we might be confronted by an angry boss when we arrived at work at 10:00 rather than at 8:30 a.m. We may also think about the delayed reinforcement we receive in the form of our paycheck. We are motivated to make our bosses happy, keep our job, and receive our paycheck. Doing those things allows us to engage in the pleasurable activities we choose in our leisure time, because our paycheck can buy us what we want. That is part of the explanation, but it is actually much more complicated. The paycheck itself is not there when we sit up in bed at 6 a.m. The paycheck is not even at work when we arrive. There is a delay in receiving the paycheck until the end of the week or month. However, even when we do get the paycheck, it is not the piece of paper on which the check is written that is pleasurable. The paycheck's value comes from its association with money. The money itself has value because of the things it is associated with, the things we can buy.

The reinforcement and motivation related to a paycheck is much more complex than that related to eating a favorite food. The pleasurable activities that are rewarding in getting a paycheck are much more removed from the behavior that earns the paycheck than is the process of digging into a bowl of ice cream. For a paycheck, there is a long history of personal experience that establishes the strong association between the paycheck, the money, and the ultimately enjoyable things one is able to do with the money. It is important to recognize that despite this complexity, the principles of reinforcement and motivation are the same as those that underlie the eating of a cookie. The essential concept is that our motivation for certain experiences will motivate us to work to gain access to them, and receiving these items or events reinforces our work and makes it likely we will do more work in the future.

Another key concept about motivation is that activities that are not inherently reinforcing can be developed into ones that are reinforcing through their association over time with pleasurable things. For example, asking to "be excused" after we finished eating was not in itself reinforcing to us as children, but when our parents praised us and let us leave the table, that small courtesy became pleasurable because it was associated with other things we liked. It is our challenge as teachers and parents to develop those kinds of associations over time for children. Sometimes, these associations happen naturally. Other times, we might need to teach them in very planned and systematic ways.

There are certainly activities in the lives of our children that may not be inherently pleasurable for them. What is the motivation for young children to learn to dress themselves or follow social rules such as saying "please" or "thank you"? Often, the motivation to engage in these tasks may be related to earning praise from an adult, having a sense of accomplishment, or successfully expressing their needs so that they can be met by others. For some children with autism, praise from a parent may not naturally be reinforcing in the same way it is for a typically developing child. This presents a challenge for teaching. It is essential that some form of motivation be established before a child can be successfully taught to engage in a behavior that is not inherently pleasurable or reinforcing. Later in this chapter we will discuss some of the ways we can begin to build new reinforcers.

Understanding the process of reinforcement is an important component of understanding motivation. Motivation is directly related to *what* is reinforcing to an individual at a *specific moment in time,* and *how valuable* that reinforcement is. These factors change from moment to moment and differ from person to person. Understanding this process will allow us to better understand natural motivation when it occurs and to better create strategies for creating motivation when the behavior we are trying to increase is not inherently pleasurable.

The Establishing Operation

For some children with autism like Maya, the process of figuring out how to motivate them to interact playfully with us, use speech to communicate, master self-help skills, and so forth is very difficult. Fortunately, thinking about the issue of motivation using the technical concept of Establishing Operation (EO) is often helpful in developing instructional programs for these youngsters. We will explain the concept of EO in detail because of its considerable value for developing an environment that provides a rich dose of reinforcement for your child. Before we look at motivation and EO specifically for the child with autism, it is helpful to explore the concept more generally as it applies to us or to children who are typical learners. Psychologist Jack Michael has written a great deal about what he originally called an *Establishing Operation.* (You may also hear the term *Motivational Operation* used to mean the same thing.) The importance of this concept is that the EO describes in a very precise way those aspects of motivation and reinforcement that are constantly changing. The EO is what makes a certain stimulus a reinforcer for a person at a specific moment in time, and tells us how this leads to specific behavior. The EO does this by identifying and describing two very specific, and technical sounding effects. One of these is the *reinforcer establishing effect* and the other is called the *evocative effect*.

The Reinforcer Establishing Effect

The reinforcer establishing effect is the process by which something becomes a reinforcer. Consider the basic example: Sue has been running outside on a very hot day and she is quite thirsty. Because of the heat and her physical exertion, water is at that moment something that she is very motivated to obtain. We might also say that water has a lot of value to Sue at that time because of her current condition, that of being hot, tired, and thirsty. It is likely that water will act as a very powerful reinforcer for Sue in her current condition. In other words, the fact that she is hot and thirsty and deprived of water has "established" water as a reinforcer.

The Evocative Effect

Given that Sue is thirsty, what will she do next? The term *evocative effect* refers to the process of how the EO (Sue's thirst) produces or *evokes* behavior that has been reinforced in the past by the desired item (water). To refer to our example, Sue is very thirsty because she has been running in the heat. Because of this, she is likely to try to get a drink of water by finding a drinking fountain or going to a store to buy a bottle of water. We can assume that Sue will engage in behavior that she knows will get her water; in other words, behavior that has been successful in the past.

In this example, we can very clearly see the two essential parts of an EO. First, water is "established" as a reinforcer, because of Sue's running and exertion in the heat. Second, behavior is *evoked* or produced that has been successful in obtaining water in the past (finding a drinking fountain).

We can use this example to think about the variables that control behavior. Why doesn't Sue spend all of her time every day walking around looking for water? The answer is that some event or circumstance has made water reinforcing at a *specific point in time*, and at other times, water does not have significant value. Water may be established as a reinforcer by running in the heat, going for a long time without water (deprivation), or eating salty pretzels or potato chips. All of these may be EOs that establish water as a reinforcer (reinforcer establishing effect).

The EO then puts behavior into action. Which behavior does Sue engage in when she is thirsty? What does she do? Sue will probably choose a behavior that has been successful in the past. That is the evocative effect. For Sue, the behavior might be to find a drinking fountain, to ask a friend for a glass of water, or to buy a drink from the vending machine. Sue will make a decision about which behavior to use based on her environment and her past experiences that have been successful. If Sue is standing in front of a drinking fountain, she is more likely to use the fountain to get her drink of water than to get in her car and drive to a convenience store to buy a bottle of water. Although both behaviors have been successful in obtaining water in the past, Sue will make a decision that takes into consideration the amount of effort that is required to get the reinforcement (the water). This is called *response effort*.

How Does All This Apply to Autism?

With that general background, let's examine how these concepts are relevant in thinking about a child with autism. For example, Zachary might enjoy watching a particular videotape, and often independently watches the video during his free time. After spending the weekend at this grandparents' house without the video, he may be very motivated to see the video after returning home. Essentially, Zachary has a level of deprivation for the specific video and the video is established as a reinforcer (the reinforcer establishing effect). Consequently, Zachary is more likely to engage in behavior that has led to him watching the video in the past (the evocative effect). Some of Zachary's choices for behavior are asking his parents for the video or looking in the entertainment cabinet for the videotape itself. If both of these methods have been consistently successful in the past at enabling him to watch the video, Zachary will be most likely to engage in the response that involves the least effort.

Alternately, imagine that Zachary has just spent two hours watching his favorite parts of the video without any interruption. After this, the video may be less likely to still be a reinforcer, or a strong reinforcer, because it has "lost" some of its value. Further, Zachary may be less likely to engage in behavior to get the video again after having watched it so much. In other words, this might be the wrong time for his parents to offer Zach the opportunity to watch the video as a reinforcer for using the toilet appropriately.

Two important variables that are related to the concept of EOs are the strength of a particular EO and the relative levels of satiation and deprivation. It is very uncommon to be either totally deprived of a specific reinforcer or totally satiated (full) of the reinforcer. Food and water are the simplest examples. It is easy to imagine being completely stuffed or totally deprived of a favorite food or drink. However, it is more common that you are somewhere in between deprivation and satiation. The concept of the EO allows us to think about that continuum when considering how reinforcing or motivating particular items or activities are likely to be. An EO is likely to be stronger when it is associated with more deprivation. Sweets or candy that are saved for special occasions are likely to be more powerful as rewards because of a greater level of deprivation, as compared to a snack that the child has free or frequent access to.

These aspects of the EO are important to consider when thinking about how well a particular item or activity will work as a motivator. You can imagine what we would call a *strong* EO. For example, if you have not eaten for twenty-four hours, you are experiencing a significant level of food deprivation. The EO that is in effect is that food is established as a reinforcer, and any behavior that is associated with obtaining food is likely to be evoked. The more deprived or hungry you are, the more effort you will expend to get to food. However, if you have been eating normally and are not deprived of food in any way (a very weak EO), it is unlikely that food will be effective to motivate behavior, particularly behavior that may involve a greater response effort.

In some instances, it becomes our job as adults to ensure that a child has an EO in place for a particular item. In Maya's case, if she eats all she wants of her two breakfast cereals before she comes to school, she is not likely to have a strong EO for them for several hours. If we want to teach her to ask for cereal, our teaching will be more effective if we do it before she is satiated. For example, Maya's parents might only give her one of the cereals she eats for breakfast, and save the other cereal for her teachers to use in school to help motivate her. If she especially likes orange juice, they might use that juice as a reinforcer for good behavior and offer Maya a less preferred beverage at other times. In other words, Maya's parents can attempt to modify her EO for some items to increase the likelihood that they are motivating.

Watching to See What Is of Interest

The first and most important step in motivating a child with autism (or any child) is to gain some understanding of what is naturally interesting and motivating for her. Carefully observing your child in a number of environments is an important part of this process. When watching your child, pay attention to what types of items or activities she approaches or engages in independently. Table 2-1 summarizes some of the variables to consider when making this assessment.

Observe how long your child's attention is held by certain activities when you are not prompting her to play and when there are no limits on playtime. Does she appear happy when engaging in the activity? It is also important to observe whether she becomes upset when an object is taken away or an activity

---

Table 2-1 | Aspects of Play and Preferred Activities to Observe

What are the common sensory aspects of toys or activities?
- Sight/Visual
- Sound/Auditory
- Touch/Tactile
- Taste/Gustatory
- Movement/Kinesthetic

What are important social aspects of activities?
- Independent activities
- Activities that involve another person or specific persons

How much time is spent in various activities?
- Without prompting
- With prompting

How does the child initiate the activities?
- Independently
- Requesting the object/activity
- Searching for items

What is the child's mood like?
- While playing
- If playing is stopped

has ended. Does she try to repeat the activity or gain access to the object again?

What types of toys does your child find interesting? Are mechanical and electronic toys interesting? Do the toys make sounds, light up, or move? What about stuffed animals or other soft toys? Do textures seem to be important? Is your child drawn to particular characters? Are there other specific interests such as letters, numbers, or shapes? Does

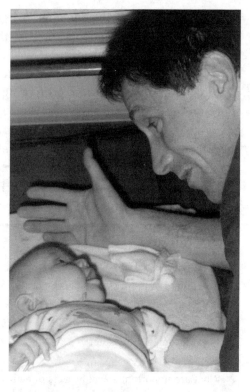

your child enjoy listening to music or watching videotapes?

What does your child do with the toys that interest her? Does she repeatedly activate and reactivate cause-and-effect toys? Does she arrange the toys and objects in specific ways? Does she explore the objects in specific ways, such as by looking at certain parts of the objects?

In addition to playing with toys, what are the other ways your child occupies her time? Does she engage in physical activities or stereotyped movements? Does she enjoy actions that let her spin, run, jump, rock, or swing? Does she incorporate objects or parts of her surroundings in this play, or does she use her own body? Does she interact or look at items other than toys in her environment, such as water, grass, street signs, or kitchen cabinets?

How does your child interact with others in her naturally occurring play? Does she seek out specific people and initiate

activities with them? Does she enjoy physical activities that involve another person, such as roughhousing, tickling, or playing
chase or other physical games?

Some of the items or activities that you observe taking up
significant portions of your child's time might not be items or activities that you can easily or ideally use to motivate her in a number of settings. For example, if a child engages in a lot of repetitive
movement, such as spinning or jumping, these activities are not as
easy to limit access to or deliver to a child to let her know she did
a good job. However, observing these activities can help you identify other possible motivators with similar characteristics. For instance, if your child likes spinning or jumping, you may be able to
use a small portable trampoline, a sit-and-spin, or rocking horse.

To begin this process of learning more about your child's
interests and motivation, you could take data over a period of
time and record her naturally occurring leisure and free time activities. A sample data sheet may look like the one shown in Table
2-2. Recording data such as this can help you to identify the most
frequently occurring activities or other patterns that may be use-

Table 2-2 | Play and Leisure Observations

Day	Time Begin	Time End	Object/Activity	Observations
Mon.	10:15 am	11:00	Watched dinosaur video	Stopped b/c video was over
Mon.	11:05	11:20	Walked around room, played with blinds on living room window	Watching sun and shadows on the wall
Mon.	11:22	11:45	Played with fire engine toy	Pushed buttons to make lights and siren go, manipulated toy ladder, doors, and wheels
Mon	11:45	12:00	Snack—cheese crackers	Pulled mom to cabinet where crackers were

Table 2-3 | Some Potentially Motivating Items

Food

- Popcorn
- Pretzels
- Potato chips
- Crackers
- French fries
- Tortilla chips
- Gummi bears
- M & M's
- Skittles
- Marshmallows
- Starbursts
- Lollipops
- Cookies
- Brownies
- Ice cream
- Pudding
- Pickles
- Olives
- Cheese
- Pepperoni

Toys/Objects

- Spinning top
- Visual timer
- Kaleidoscope
- Prism
- Books
- Letters
- Numbers
- Light-up toys
- Bubbles
- Keyboard
- Musical phone
- CD player
- Musical/sound books
- See 'N Say
- Play-Doh
- Koosh ball

Activities

- Swinging in air
- Lifted up
- Spinning around
- Tickling
- Chasing
- Hugging
- Kisses
- Back rubs
- Cheering
- Singing
- Trampoline
- Rocking horse
- Sand play
- Rice play
- Water play
- Swing

ful. At the Douglass Center, we often ask parents to complete a checklist of possible motivators. Parents are given an extensive list of items or activities that may be common motivators. This may help guide your observations as you begin to establish a list. Table 2-3 gives a sample of the types of items that may be included on this type of observation and assessment.

The Harder to Please Child

Sometimes it is difficult to identify a list of potential motivators for an individual child. Like Maya, your child may have a very narrow range of interests. She may spend the majority of her time engaging in stereotyped behavior that is repetitive and interferes with interactions with other items or activities in her environment. In cases like this, watching your child might not give you enough information about a range of motivators that you will be able to use effectively. As Maya's parents did, you or your child's teacher will need to find ways to control your child's access to those few items or activities that operate as reinforcers. This will enable you or the teacher to work with your child's EO.

Often, a child may show interest in novel items that are presented to her, although she may not initially seek these items or activities out in her own leisure time. A child may not have enough experience with a particular item for those items to be established as possible reinforcers. At these times, the child may require some guided exposure or experience with an item to become familiar with its potentially reinforcing properties. In other cases, a child may be particularly interested in or distracted by one or two extremely motivating items, preventing her from showing interest in other potentially motivating items.

Assessing Your Child's Interests

A number of clinicians and researchers in the field have developed special assessments to help identify preferences in individuals who may not spontaneously demonstrate interest in a range of items. These assessments involve setting up specific environments and choices, and then carefully observing a child's behavior under different conditions. Watching a child's behavior can give clues about new items or activities that may be reinforcing. These assessments are also important to consider when reevaluating a child's preferences. As we know, a child's preferences and interests change over time, and even from moment to moment. Borrowing strategies from these assessments and even conducting mini-assessments on a frequent basis can help a parent or teacher to be aware of new and changing interests for the child. However, these assessments do take time. If your child has many clear preferences, you may not wish to pursue this process. On the other hand, if you are hard pressed to find potential reinforcers, it will be worth the effort.

The Pace Method

One type of assessment was developed by a group of researchers led by Dr. Gary Pace (Pace, Ivancic, Edwards, Iwata, & Page, 1985). In this assessment, a set of sixteen possible items is first identified by people who are familiar with the child and her behavior. The items to be tested may include things the child has previously shown an interest in on other occasions. The items may also be novel materials, or may be items that have some characteristics that might interest a specific child. For example, if your child has shown an interest in brightly colored objects and often brings objects to her eyes while playing with them, toys or objects such as prisms, kaleidoscopes, or colored sunglasses might be introduced. Typically, items chosen should be relatively easy to present to a child and practical to use as a reinforcer.

The sixteen items are then divided into four groups of four items each. The assessment is conducted over eight sessions. Each session assesses one of the groups of four items, and each group is assessed in two separate sessions. In the first session, a teacher or parent presents the child with one item at a time and records whether the child "approaches" or plays with the item. If she does, she is allowed to play with it for a few seconds. If the child does not interact with the item, the instructor might gently prompt her to touch or hold the item, or activate it to show the child how it works. The child is then given another chance to approach the item on her own.

After presenting the first item, the instructor goes through the other three items the same way. Next, he or she presents all four items one at a time again, but in a different order, with only one item visible at a time. During each session, the child is exposed to the four items in one group five times. By the time all eight sessions are finished, the child has been able to try each of the sixteen items ten times.

The instructor takes careful data to keep track of whether the child approaches the item on her own during those ten trials. The most preferred items would be those that she approached the greatest percentage of times. For example, if a child reaches for and plays with the spinning top eight out of the ten times it is presented to her, it would have a score of 80 percent. Dr. Pace and his colleagues showed that items that were approached 80 percent or more of the time were very likely to be effective as reinforcers. Table 2-4 on the next page shows sample data for a group of four items using the Pace procedure.

The Pace stimulus preference procedure is a systematic way to introduce new items to your child that may be potential reinforcers. This is especially useful for children who may not naturally show interest in a variety of different items. Of course, you will not know if a particular item will act as a reinforcer until you see that it can effectively increase behavior. And, as we learned before, the item may not be a reinforcer at a specific moment in time if there is no Establishing Operation (EO) in effect.

The Pace system was quite helpful in determining some potential reinforcers for Maya. Careful observation identified several different visual items that were of considerable interest to her, including a kaleidoscope, spinning top, and a game with blinking lights that went on and off in a pattern. These items were introduced into teaching sessions and offered a broader range of appealing items to motivate Maya's performance than had been available in the past.

Table 2-4 | Sample Data for an Assessment Based on the Pace Procedure

Group 1	Trial 1	Trial 2	Trial 3	Trial 4	Trial 5	Trial 6	Trial 7	Trial 8	Trial 9	Trial 10
	Session 1					Session 2				
Prism	A ✔ R P+ P-	A ✔ R P+ P-	A R P+ ✔ P-	A ✔ R P+ P-	A ✔ R P+ P-	A ✔ R P+ P-	A ✔ R P+ P-	A R P+ ✔ P-	A ✔ R P+ P-	A R ✔ P+ P-
Top	A ✔ R P+ P-	A ✔ R P+ P-	A R P+ ✔ P-	A ✔ R P+ P-	A R ✔ P+ P-	A ✔ R P+ P-	A ✔ R P+ P-	A ✔ R P+ P-	A ✔ R P+ P-	A ✔ R P+ P-
Licorice	A R P+ ✔ P-	A R P+ ✔ P-	A R P+ ✔ P-	A ✔ R P+ P-	A R ✔ P+ P-	A ✔ R P+ P-	A R P+ ✔ P-	A ✔ R P+ P-	A R P+ P- ✔	A R P+ ✔ P-
Play-doh	A R P+ P- ✔	A R ✔ P+ P-	A R P+ ✔ P-	A ✔ R P+ P-	A ✔ R P+ P-	A R P+ ✔ P-	A R P+ ✔ P-	A ✔ R P+ P-	A R P+ ✔ P-	A ✔ R P+ P-

A = Approach, R = Reject, P+ = Approach after prompting, P- = Reject after prompting

The Fisher Method

Other procedures in addition to the Pace method have been developed in order to assess a child's preference for items and to determine how reinforcing each item is compared to other items. For example, your child may like crackers, but crackers are no competition for cookies! So, while the Pace procedure can help identify what new things your child might like, another procedure can be helpful to determine which things your child might like more than others.

One assessment of this type was designed by a group of researchers led by Dr. Wayne Fisher (Fisher, Piazza, Bowman, Hagopian, Owen, & Slevin, 1992). In this assessment, sixteen items are identified in the same manner as in the Pace procedure described above. A grid is established in which each item is paired with another item to be tested. The grid is arranged so that every possible combination of items can be assessed, for a total of 120 pairs. The child is presented with a pair of items, and an observer records which item the child reaches for or manipu-

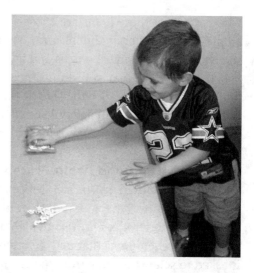

lates out of the pair. There is no need to ask the child what she wants—the choices can be presented without the use of language, which is an advantage when working with a child who has limited language. If the child does not show any interest in either object, the clinician might demonstrate each object's use or give the child a sample of each item before presenting the pair again.

Based on the percentage of times a particular object is chosen, the items can be rated in a general order of preference. So, although you might already know that your child likes bubbles, books, and cars, using the Fisher procedure you can find out

Table 2-5 | Sample Data for an Assessment Based on Fisher's Procedure

X Bubbles	☐ Car	☐ Car	X Book
☐ Bubbles	X Book	X Car	☐ Popcorn
X Bubbles	☐ Popcorn	X Book	☐ Popcorn

Bubbles chosen 2/3 times = 66%

Book chosen 3/3 times = 100%

Car chosen 1/3 times = 33%

Popcorn chosen 0/3 times = 0%

whether any of these items are chosen more than others. For example, you can offer her bubbles and a wind-up car and see which she chooses. Then offer bubbles and a book, and finally the book and the car. Note that you do not need to use sixteen items to follow this procedure. See the sample data sheet in Figure 2-5 on the previous page for an example of what results might look like with just four items (instead of all sixteen).

The DeLeon and Iwata Procedure

Other researchers, Drs. Iser DeLeon and Brian Iwata (1996), designed an alternate method of systematically assessing an individual's preferences. In this model, a child is presented with an array of seven items that may be interesting or appealing. She is asked to select one item from the group. Each time she demonstrates interest in an item, she is allowed to play with or manipulate it for a brief period. After that, the object is removed and the order of the remaining objects is rearranged. The child is then asked to choose again, and the procedure is repeated until all items are gone. After the child has chosen all of the items, the session is completed.

Later that same day or on another day, all seven items are presented to the child again. The entire procedure is repeated for a total of five sessions, with no more than one or two sessions per day.

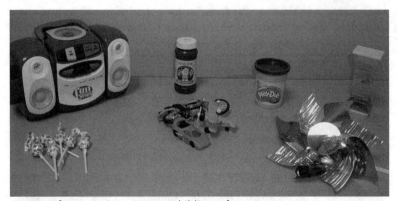

An array for assessing a young child's preferences.

After completing this assessment, you will have information about the items that were chosen first and last in order to make some comparisons and predictions about the possible strength of some items as reinforcers. For example, if your child selects a whistle first in all five sessions, the whistle might be a very strong reinforcer for her. On the other hand, if she takes the a wind-up toy last (seventh) in four out of five sessions, then it may be a weaker reinforcer. Table 2-6 gives an example of possible data using DeLeon and Iwata's procedure.

Table 2-6 | Sample Data for an Assessment Based on DeLeon & Iwata's Procedure

	Wind-up toy	Hand-held fan	Rubber ball	Reflective sticker	Graham crackers	Oreos	Whistle
Trial 1	7th	5th	6th	4th	3rd	2nd	1st
Trial 2	7th	6th	5th	4th	2nd	3rd	1st
Trial 3	7th	4th	6th	5th	3rd	2nd	1st
Trial 4	5th	6th	7th	4th	3rd	2nd	1st
Trial 5	7th	5th	6th	2nd	4th	3rd	1st
Average	6.6	5.2	6	3.8	3	2.4	1

Some Considerations in Assessing Your Child

With all these procedures, it is important to remember that compiling a list of items your child enjoys and "ranking" these in order of preference does not guarantee that these items will be effective as reinforcers and capable of motivating behavior at any given moment. Have you ever heard a teacher say that a child "just won't work for any of her reinforcers" or that a child "is not motivated by any of her rewards?" We know that not all pleasurable activities are motivating at all times. What delights us one day may have less appeal the next. What makes a particular item a reinforcer at a specific point in time is the EO.

Identifying a list of your child's preferences is therefore just a *first step* in being able to motivate her to engage in important be-

haviors. If a teacher identifies a list of preferences and stops there, she is likely to run into problems, as we described above, when the reinforcers don't work. However, having a longer list of possibilities will be helpful, because if some potential rewards don't seem to be working as reinforcers, others may. Understanding the EO allows us to learn more about when a preference is established as a reinforcer and when it is not, and, by definition, when it will work to motivate behavior, and when it will not. We will learn more about using EOs to our advantage in later chapters.

You may run into a number of challenges when trying to set up and conduct reinforcer assessments with your child. For example, what if your child seems completely disinterested or won't participate or attend to the assessment procedure itself? There are a few different things to consider in this case. First, you may need to examine the items that you have selected to use in your reinforcer assessment and see whether you need to include different items that will better capture your child's attention and interest. You may also need to consider the setting where you are assessing your child. The room or space you are using may be too large or too distracting, and a smaller environment might be easier to begin with. Also, you may be able to adjust the format of the assessment. For instance, it is not necessary for your child to sit at a desk or table to participate. Items may be placed on tables, in bins, or on the floor, and your child can approach the items she wants. This way, a preference assessment can be conducted for a child even if she does not sit down and readily attend to an instructor.

Sometimes it may be difficult to find a pattern when looking at the data about which items your child chose. If so, it might not seem that she has clear preferences. Then again, if she has chosen many of the items, it may be that she has a wide range of interests, or enjoys novelty. This is important and helpful information that can be used when working to motivate your child. If your child has many interests or is interested in novel items, it will be helpful to use a large number of frequently changing items as reinforcement.

For the purposes of a preference assessment, it is not important that your child play with the toy or object in any particular or "correct" way. The goal of these procedures is to find out what she likes to do. If she prefers to play with a certain item in a potentially dangerous way or some other unacceptable way, you would probably choose not to use this item to motivate or reinforce your child's behavior, and you probably would not include such items in the assessments. For other items, you may want to weigh both the advantages and disadvantages of using an item your child "plays" with in an idiosyncratic way. For example, your child may choose to play with a book nine out of ten times it is presented, but plays with the book by repeatedly fanning the pages, rather than reading or looking at the pictures. In this case, the book is still considered a strong preference for your child. It is up to you to decide whether you are comfortable with using books as one of the ways to motivate your child. In the early stages of teaching, you may be willing to compromise by allowing some of this atypical behavior to help motivate your child to learn new skills. Once new skills have been established, it may be easier to find newer or more "appropriate" reinforcers.

Building New Reinforcers

Even after we are able to identify a long list of items that a child seems to enjoy, the job is not finished. Relying completely on treats or toys may be effective in the early stages of teaching, but it is not ideal for the long term. Expanding the possible pool of reinforcers will be an advantage and will increase flexibility. A greater number of possible reinforcers will mean that there may be a greater likelihood of identifying an EO in effect for one of the reinforcers at any given point in time. In addition, by creating new reinforcers, you may be able to increase the range of more typical things that could work as reinforcers. That is, some of the rewards that work for your other children or your child's classmates may also become reinforcers for your child with autism. In addition, as your child grows older, you will want to make sure you are using reinforcers that are age appropriate. Items that were strong reinforcers for a young child, such as tickles or being picked up, will no longer be appropriate or feasible for a school-aged child or adolescent. It will be helpful to begin thinking early about establishing new rewards that are more age appropriate, such as high-fives or hand-held video games.

One of the most important concepts in establishing new reinforcers is *pairing*. This refers to the process of pairing something that is known to be a reinforcer with something that is not yet thought of as a reinforcer. For example, a child who loves to be picked up and swung in the air may frequently approach a particular family member or babysitter who often swings her. However, she may initially ignore a new teacher or babysitter who has not yet been paired with this fun activity. Once the new person creates a history of approaching the child, holding out her arms, and lifting her up to swing her around, the new person will come to be associated with the rewarding activity of being swung in the air. Often, this association does not take place automatically and may require frequent occurrences.

One of the most important steps in the process of pairing is to think about how you can establish important people in your child's life as reinforcers, by linking them with things that she enjoys. For Maya's parents and teacher, pairing themselves with reinforcement became a high priority as they worked to engage her in learning. For example, two of the few things that Maya enjoyed included olives and rolling rubber balls on the floor. Ahmed and Lily made an effort to sit down with Maya and offer her small bits of olive, or bring her to a place that would become a work area and give her small bits of olive and rubber balls to play with. The Browns did this throughout the day, in five- to ten-minute sessions. In this way, Maya came to associate sitting down with her parents with things that she already enjoyed. In other words, she began to learn that the sight of Ahmed or Lily coming to sit with her meant that "good things were coming!"

Objects can also be paired with other objects. For example, a gold star sticker on your child's worksheet might not be particularly meaningful at first. However, think of the things that become paired with that gold star. The star is paired with praise ("Wow! Look what a great job you did. I'm so proud of you!"), and the star might also be paired with special treats or privileges ("Let's go get ice cream because you did such a nice job on your homework"). These associations seem to happen naturally and easily with many typically developing children, but it is important to plan this type of pairing explicitly for learners with autism, as explained in Chapter 1.

Social praise and interaction with others, while naturally reinforcing for many children, may not be enjoyable for individuals with autism. To whatever extent possible, it will surely benefit your child with autism to pair social praise with other reinforcers so that praise may become a reinforcer in its own right over time. You should also be aware, however, that the items your child finds motivating may be very different from what her peers find motivating. Working with individuals with autism involves recognizing these differences and respecting the ways in which they are unique.

Money is a very common example of something that is not initially valued on its own, but that becomes very valuable when it is systematically paired with countless other enjoyable things. These are the same principles that apply to establishing reinforcers for children with autism. Something that is not a reinforcer on its own can be paired over and over with an established reinforcer until the association is created. Sometimes these associations need to be taught very specifically and with a lot of repetition. Teaching your child the value of money or other tokens will be an important step in developing a range of reinforcers over time. This concept will be addressed in Chapter 5.

Investing the time and energy to establish new reinforcers will be an important part of preparing to teach and motivate your child. Over time, the new item may become a reinforcer on its own, and may no longer need to be paired. To test whether the new item acts as a reinforcer when it is presented on its own, you would look at the criteria that make an item a reinforcer. If you deliver the item after your child makes a certain response, does that response continue or increase in the future? If so, it is likely that the new item is acting as a reinforcer. Whether or not your child learns to value the same things that other children find reinforcing, it will always be important to continue pairing items and developing new reinforcers over time.

Summary

This chapter introduced the fundamental principles related to motivation: reinforcement and the EO. We described the ways reinforcing items and events help to increase behavior in children with autism spectrum disorders, and we also explained how the EO works to establish events or items as reinforcers. Identifying reinforcers and the impact of EOs on the learners we work with is essential to our efforts in motivating children with autism to learn. Children's reinforcers are unique and constantly changing. We discussed ways to make careful and systematic observations to learn more about the possible reinforcers for the children with whom we work. In addition, we described special assessments to help identify reinforcers for learners with narrow interests or preferences that are hard to identify. Finally, we explored the concept of pairing—that is, creating new reinforcers by linking them with established ones. Establishing new reinforcers is an important way to expand the range of potential motivators and increase the success of our teaching efforts.

References

DeLeon, I. G. & Iwata, B. A. (1996). Evaluation of a multiple stimulus presentation format for assessing reinforcer preferences. *Journal of Applied Behavior Analysis*, 29(4), 519-33.

Fisher, W. W., Piazza, C.C., Bowman, L. P., Hagopian, L. P., Owen, J. C. & Slevin, I. (1992) A comparison of two approaches for identifying reinforcers for persons with severe and profound disabilities. *Journal of Applied Behavior Analysis*, 25(2), 491-98.

Michael, J. (1982). Distinguishing between discriminative and motivational functions of stimuli. *Journal of the Experimental Analysis of Behavior*, 32, 149-55.

Pace, G. M., Ivancic, M. T., Edwards, G. L., Iwata, B.A. & Page, T. J. (1985). Assessment of stimulus preference and reinforcer value with profoundly retarded individuals. *Journal of Applied Behavior Analysis*, 18(3), 249-55.

3 | Mand Training: "Give Me That"

The Dunn Family

Max Dunn, a sober-faced boy of three years, was red in the face and howling as his parents tried to get him to put down a tiny, shabby piece of blue cloth from his baby blanket, and hold up his arms so they could put a t-shirt over his head. Much of Max's day was spent either protesting when his parents asked him to stop one of his stereotypic routines, or else rocking his whole body, waving his hands, or pushing the rewind or fast forward button on the VCR remote control. On rare occasions when he really seemed to want something, Max might use one of the half dozen words in his vocabulary, including "juice," "push," "up," and "open." Ordinarily, however, a shrieking "NO" was the only word that he used to communicate with.

Life in the Dunn family was often difficult. Max's six-year-old sister, Rosie, was afraid of her brother and avoided him when she could. His parents, Wayne and Beverly, felt totally ineffectual in dealing with their son's needs and were often angry and frustrated. They realized they were in urgent need of a way to "hook" Max into wanting to be with them, but had no idea what to do. Nothing they had tried seemed to help. It was as though their son hardly knew they were there.

The Dunns had contacted their local school district to find a suitable program for Max and were encouraged to discover that the district had a preschool class for young children with autism. The program used the principles of Applied Behavior Analysis and teachers would work with Max on a one-to-one basis for five hours a day. They also planned to provide home support and parent training for the Dunn family.

Shortly after Max entered the preschool class, his new teacher, Gary Zane, had a conference with Wayne and Beverly to discuss some first steps in Max's education. He told them that based on his initial interactions with Max and the assessment he had been doing in class, they were going to start their work with Max using a procedure called "Mand Training." The purpose of this was to help Max discover that learning was fun and that when he asked for what he wanted, he could get those items. This would lay the groundwork for more language learning and more social interaction, and ultimately might help reduce his difficult behavior. They were also going to do a careful analysis of Max's difficult-to-manage behaviors and try to determine whether any environmental changes could be made to reduce his frustration and thereby minimize his tantrums. Gary also promised that as soon as he found some techniques that were helpful in the classroom, he would meet with the Dunns to teach them how to use the same procedures at home.

It was the first glimmer of hope the Dunns had felt in some months and they were ready to try anything that might help Max and restore their family life to some semblance of normalcy and comfort.

Discussion

The challenges that Max Dunn's autism created for him and for his parents are not unusual. Although not every child is as hard to reach as Max, many youngsters with autism pose significant demands in the lives of parents and siblings. Perhaps even more distressing, Max's behavior reflects the perplexity and frustration faced by many children and adults with autism who do not know how to interact with other people in a way that will get their needs met. The tantrums, aggression, and other problematic behaviors of these youngsters often reflect their utter inability to get what they want in any other way.

The hopeful news is that for many children, learning enough language to communicate their basic needs provides them with a viable alternative to disruptive behavior. One very potent approach to teaching children the value of communication is a procedure called "mand training." Giving a detailed description of this teaching method is the goal of this chapter. We have included mand training in this book because it is a way to help a child learn to name the things that he finds reinforcing.

What Is a Mand?

We mand all the time. Each time we say, "Tell me what you want for dinner," "Pass the meat please," or "Give me a few minutes," we are manding. That is, we are asking for something. It might be a request for an item such as ice cream or a book, or it might be a mand in which we ask someone for information (e.g., "Where do you want to go on vacation?"). That is the essence of this technical term—a mand is a request or instruction.

We have the distinguished psychologist B.F. Skinner to thank for the concept of the mand. Some years ago he wrote a book about verbal behavior in which he analyzed the different forms in which we communicate (Skinner, 1957). He was interested not in the grammatical form of language, but in the functions that our language serves. Rather than looking at verbs and nouns, he asked, "What are different ways in which we use language to communicate?" Skinner described a number of different functions. One of these was the "mand" (as in com<u>mand</u> or de<u>mand</u>). Other basic functions include "tacts" or names of things (as in con<u>tact</u>ing the environment), and "intraverbals" or back-and-forth exchanges between people. An example of a tact would be when a parent asks, "What is this?" and the child responds, "Bear." In that example, the parent manded for information ("What is this?") and the child tacted the object ("bear"). An intraverbal exchange might consist of one child saying to the other, "I saw my Uncle Jim, the Marine, last night. He was wearing his uniform," and the other child saying, "Wow, that is so cool."

Table 3-1 defines the terms mand, tact, and intraverbal. In Table 3-2 you will find a short quiz you can take to be certain that you understand the basic concept of these three terms.

Two very creative psychologists, Mark Sundberg and James Partington (1998), took the theoretical writings of Skinner on verbal behavior and transformed them into a curriculum for teaching language to children with autism, called Natural Environment Training (NET). Many people who work with children with autism find this framework very helpful in organizing language instruction. Their book, *Teaching Language to Children with Autism or Other Developmental Disabilities,* is user friendly and appropriate across a fair range of language learners.

Our focus in this chapter is on teaching children with little if any communicative speech to use mands to express their needs. We will not address how to move beyond mands to other forms of language because our focus in this book is on motivation, but the interested reader will find considerable help with the broader topic of language instruction in Sundberg's and Partington's book.

Table 3-1 | Some Basic Vocabulary

Intraverbal: A response to someone else's language, as in a conversational interaction.

Mand: A request for an item, for an experience, or for information.

Natural Environment Training (NET): The language instruction approach of Sundberg and Partington (1998).

S^D: The abbreviation for "discriminative stimulus." An S^D is some event such as a request by a parent (e.g., "What do you want?") that is a cue for the child to respond and indicates that reinforcement will be available for the response.

Tact: Naming items in the environment.

Verbal Behavior: An examination of the impact or functions of language including mands, tacts, and intraverbals. Based on the book of that name by Skinner (1957).

Table 3-2 | Name That Word

For each of the following exchanges, label the parent and/or child statement as a mand, tact, or intraverbal.

1. Parent: "John, come here."
2. Parent: "What is this?" Child: "A cup."
3. Child: "Want gummy bear." Parent: "Which color?"
4. Child: "What are we doing today?" Parent: "Let's go to the beach." Child: "The beach is fun!"
5. Child: "Moon" (while pointing to moon). Parent: "Yes, I see the moon too."

Answers:
1. Parent: Mand
2. Parent: Mand (for information); Child: Tact (and intraverbal too because he's answering a question)
3. Child: Mand; Parent: Mand (for information and intraverbal too because he's answering a question)
4. Child: Mand (for information); Parent: Intraverbal; Child: Intraverbal
5. Child: Tact (maybe a mand too if he wants the moon!); Parent: Intraverbal (and tact too if the parent is looking at the moon)

Who Needs to Mand?

Any learner with autism, mental retardation, or other disability that intrudes on the learning of language can benefit from learning to mand. For many children, manding will be a spoken behavior, but for some it may be a manual sign, pointing to a picture, or handing another person a picture of an item. These are all "verbal" behaviors because they all communicate, whether through vocal speech, manual sign, or picture symbols. We will focus here on teaching children to mand with speech, but if your child has no speech, you may want to consider using manual sign or pictures instead. See Sundberg and Partington (1998) for help with using manual signs to mand and see *A Picture's Worth: PECS and Other Visual Communication Strategies in Autism* by Andy Bondy and Lori Frost (2001) for information about working with picture symbols to teach language, including mands to children who do not yet have speech.

In addition to being an essential part of the instruction of very young children with autism, teaching manding is appropriate for older children, adolescents, and adults who did not learn to mand when they were younger. A decade ago, language instruction for children with autism often failed to put enough emphasis on initiation by the student. As a result, many students learned to label (tact) when asked, but not to mand. Fortunately, it is never too late to introduce this skill to a learner. We have adults at our Center who have done very well in learning to mand. If you are introducing manding to an adolescent or adult with autism, you can follow the same basic programs, just making sure the materials you use are age appropriate.

When Do You Teach Manding?

We recommend that manding be introduced very early in a child's instruction. This is especially true if the child has little functional speech and is using a variety of maladaptive behaviors to communicate instead of speech. We want him to learn that being with his teacher is the niftiest thing that can happen to him because he gets access to great opportunities, and that if he uses mands to make requests he gains control over what happens to him. The child who can say, "cookie" when he wants a cookie does not have to have a tantrum to express his utter frustration at not being able to let us know what he wants.

Not only does the child who can mand come to experience time with his teacher and parents as highly rewarding and discover that language is power, he also has an interpersonal exchange when he mands. He is asking his teacher or his father for a cookie and they are providing it, along with warmth and praise. In addition, learning to mand can form the foundation for learning to tact (label) and receptively identify objects, launching him on a path to learning more complex language. Manding is very cool behavior!

How Do You Teach Manding?

The first step in teaching manding to a child of limited verbal ability is to identify one or more items or experiences that appear to be motivating for him. As we described in Chapter 2, sometimes this can be done through careful observations of the things a child seems to prefer, and sometimes we may have to do a more formal assessment of his preferences by offering him a range of items and seeing which he consistently selects. If you have not found some items that attract your child's interest, you should follow the suggestions in Chapter 2 to identify items he might enjoy.

To continue the story of Max Dunn that opened this chapter, his parents ultimately determined that one thing Max very much enjoyed at home was going on the swing in his backyard. They decided to use that activity as the context for teaching Max his first spoken mand. However, because Max's level of resistance was very high, they had to begin with an even more basic first step of teaching him that compliance with their simple instructions would result in good things happening to him. Sundberg and Partington (1998) refer to the process of establishing a working relationship as building rapport and compliance training. If your child is cooperative and follows your instructions to the best of his ability, you can skip this section on teaching compliance and move directly to mand training. However, if your child is often resistant as Max Dunn was, you will want to lay the groundwork for mand training by showing him that being with you and following simple directions can be highly reinforcing.

Teaching Compliance

In Chapter 2 we discussed at some length the concept of the Establishing Operation (EO). In that chapter, we described the need to identify items that might be reinforcing for your child at the current time and to use that motivation to encourage him to make a response to obtain the item he wishes. For example, Max often wanted to go outside and be pushed on the swing, so that was the setting in which the Dunns decided to work on rapport and compliance. As Sundberg and Partington (1998) point out, there has to be a reason for a child to be compliant. That reason is that doing what an adult asks results in more and better reinforcements than he might obtain via tantrums, aggression, or not responding to the request. Your child's initial effort to comply should result in very easy access to the reinforcer. In other words, for minimal effort he should receive a significant reinforcer. Later in teaching you will start to ask for more work in exchange for a reinforcer, but initially, as you are establishing rapport, the effort should be minimal and the reinforcement substantial.

The first step in teaching compliance is making the parent or teacher an attractive partner. If a child can have more fun when she sits in the sandbox with the sand dribbling between her fingers than she can when she interacts with an adult, she is likely to prefer to continue her stereotypic fingering of the sand. In Max's case, he was more likely to play with the buttons on the remote control than to sit next to his parents to look at a book, put on his shirt, or do many of the things they wanted him to do. However, because Max loved the swing, that was where they decided to begin making themselves fun partners.

One morning when Max's sister was at a friend's house for a play date, Beverly Dunn launched the project she and her husband had planned with Max's teacher. She waited until Max was standing by the swing set, pushing the swing back and forth in a lackadaisical fashion and then went over to him and said, "Up. Go swing?" Max held out his arms and Beverly lifted Max into the swing. Then, standing in front of Max so he could see her and link her to his pleasure, Beverly gave the swing a push and as she did so, said, "Push!" and laughed. Max appeared delighted to be in the swing and his mother pushed the swing several times, each time saying "Push." This word had been chosen because on a few occasions Max had said "pu" when he was on the swing, so it seemed like a response that he might learn quickly.

Because Max became so readily engaged in the swinging and appeared to be having fun, Beverly decided to see if she could move a tiny step toward compliance. After a few minutes the swing began to slow and Beverly said, "Max, what do you want? Say 'Push.'" Max, to her profound delight, did say "pu." Thrilled, Beverly said, "Yes, push" as she gave the swing several good pushes. She continued the game for several minutes. Then, when she saw that Max was losing interest, she decided to stop while she was ahead, saying, "One more push and then it's snack time." As Max slid off the swing, she brought out a small plastic bag with one of his favorite cookies and juice and sat with Max while he enjoyed his snack.

Although the episode was brief, perhaps ten minutes in total, Beverly had been able to create a condition in which Max had much more fun than he had experienced before she came over to lift him onto the swing and push him. She also was able to get him to say "pu" on several occasions and then ended the session with a much-coveted snack. It was an excellent beginning for building rapport and the start of a very simple mand. It would take many more sessions before Max was fully compliant and manding was established, but such long-term goals grow from small beginnings.

Although not every child responds as well and as quickly as Max did, children with autism typically do become engaged in the process of manding and learning compliance because they are being reinforced for very modest demands with experiences that they find highly attractive. Identifying potent reinforcers and making small demands that are well within the child's capabilities are key to success.

Sundberg and Partington (1998) recommend that in establishing early mands the instructor have control over something that the child very much wants and that the child be at least mildly cooperative. Max's mother did a good job of creating those conditions. Max could not swing without her help and it was something he very much enjoyed, so Beverly was in control of the activity. She had also taken time to build some rapport with Max and he was being responsive to her at the point when she asked him to say, "push" and he responded with "pu." Sundberg and Partington also point out that the crucial thing at this early stage of mand training is for your child to do something because you ask him to do it. Beverly asked Max to say "push" and he did. This is a first step toward teaching him to follow the instructions of adults.

If Max were not able to say "pu" and did not say it with some frequency, Beverly might have tried to get him to use a manual sign for "push." If necessary, she could have helped him form the sign by manipulating his fingers. Or she might have taught him to hand her a picture of a swing to request the swing. Beyond providing a clear vocal model and reinforcing attempts to speak, it is difficult to help a child say a word. Because you can provide a physical prompt for forming a sign or handing over a picture, you will want to consider using a few simple signs or pictures as an early mode of communication if your child has no speech. Using these methods, you can teach him to mand and help establish a good working relationship.

For some children who have a very limited repertoire of behavior, the simple gesture of holding out his hand or reaching for an item you are holding might be sufficient as an initial behavior. The decision about using signs versus pictures for nonvocal communication is a complex one that you should make in consultation with an expert in Applied Behavior Analysis or an experienced speech and language therapist who has extensive experience with children on the autism spectrum.

As Sundberg and Partington (1998) point out, a key achievement in the early stages of building rapport is for your child to approach you or the teacher rather than leaving the scene when you appear. Wanting to be around an adult suggests that your child has started to understand that good things will happen in that situation. So, take this process slowly and be aware that you are building a solid relationship that delights your child. Although not every interaction will be reinforcing, there should be more pleasure than distress in the teaching context.

Teaching the Initial Mand

At the Douglass Center, we develop detailed, written programs to help parents teach their child new skills, including manding. These programs always include the same components so we can make sure parents know how to work with their child step by step to learn the new skill. If you want to try teaching your child or student to mand, you may want to use this same format. The elements included in our program plans are described in the section below.

Elements of Teaching Programs

1. **Target Behavior:** The term *target behavior* names the specific behavior you are planning to teach.
2. **Behavioral Definition:** A behavioral definition is a very precise description of the behavior, written in such a way that two or more people who use the program will know exactly what they are teaching.
3. **Description of Program:** A description of a program tells the teacher the details of how to provide the information the child will need to respond and what to do when the child makes a correct or incorrect response.
4. **S^D for Target Behavior:** The term S^D refers to the cue or instruction that is given to the child. For example, "Stand up," "Come here," or "Say push."
5. **Consequences:** Delivering a reinforcement for a correct behavior or verbal feedback for an error are examples of consequences for a behavior.
6. **Data Collection:** It is important to keep records of a child's performance, and in the Data Collection section, we describe how those records will be taken.

There is nothing magical about writing a teaching program. With a little bit of training from someone who has done it, most parents can learn to write programs for their own child. However, it can be time consuming, and, to the extent it is possible, you will want to rely on your child's teacher or consultant to create your programs. It is more important to implement these programs than it is to be able to write them.

The Dunns' Program

Figure 3-1 shows the first written program that the Dunns used to teach Max to mand. At this point in his training, Max was receiving both spoken and visual prompts. Notice that in addition to the reinforcement of being pushed on the swing, his mother or father would also praise him, saying things such as "Good boy," or "Great saying 'push.'" This was done to pair the words of praise with the reinforcing experience of being on the swing, in hopes that his parents' praise would gradually become reinforcing to

---

Fig. 3-1 | Teaching Initial Mand with Full Prompts

Child: Max   **Teacher:** Mother/father

Target Behavior: Manding for push on swing with spoken and visual prompts.

Behavioral Definition: When asked, "What do you want," with teacher providing spoken prompt ("say push") and visual prompt (holding up hands toward swing and making pushing gesture) Max will echo, "pu."

Description of Program: Help Max get on swing and give him a few preliminary pushes to start the rhythm of swinging. With each pushing gesture say, "push." Teacher stands in front of Max so he can see her and connect motion with her movement. Ensure he is attending to pushes. After a few seconds of pushing and when Max is oriented toward teacher and appears engaged, allow swing to slow. As it slows, if he shows any reaction such as mild agitation or noises, say to Max, "What do you want?" Immediately provide full spoken prompt, "Say push," and make a pushing gesture. When Max makes approximation of word, give the swing several pushes before allowing it to slow again. Repeat the cycle several times, taking care to ensure he does not appear to become bored or distressed about speed of

Max as he came to associate it with pleasurable events such as swinging or favorite snacks.

Notice that one component of the program in Figure 3-1 concerns data collection. Keeping records of a child's performance helps us adjust our teaching to ensure that he is making progress and to move on to a new program when a specified goal is met for the current program. To make data collection easy, the programs in the present chapter require only a sample of a child's performance. During the first three trials of each session, Max's parent would make a hash mark on a piece of paper to note whether he responded correctly. In this initial program, that meant determining whether he said an approximation of "push" when given the spoken and visual prompt to do so. A "+" is recorded for each correct response and a "-" for each error. In later programs, as the prompts were

---

swinging. When he makes no indication of wanting more pushes by increased motor or vocal activity or by saying, "pu," it is time to end that session and go on to snack time. Initially give two or three pushes after each request and then gradually decrease to one push. Do not allow him to become bored, if you can avoid it.

S^D for Target Behavior: "What do you want?" with spoken ("say push") and visual (pushing gesture toward swing) prompts.

Consequences: Reinforcement should be inherent in the action of being pushed on swing. Pair this with praise for "nice asking," "good talking." You can say other happy words while you push, such as "This is fun." Be sure words are ones he understands and keep it simple and very enthusiastic.

Data Collection: Probe Max's performance on the first three trials of each session and write down the score. After Max is on the swing and before giving initial push, ask "What do you want?" with spoken and visual prompts and record his response. Give him a "+" for each correct response and a "-" when he fails to respond. If Max does say an approximation of "push," then provide push and repeat probe two more times. On the first and second probe trials, only push him if he says "push." On the third probe, if he fails to say "push" you can use this as a teaching trial. If he does request "push" three times in a row with full prompts, it is time to move to next program, which will reduce visual prompt.

removed, a "+" required a response without a specific prompt. See below for an example of a data collection sheet.

Table 3-3 | Sample Data Sheet

Date	Trial 1	Trial 2	Trial 3	Total +
10/4	+	-	-	1
10/5	-	-	+	1
10/6	+	-	+	2
10/7	+	+	-	2
10/8	+	+	+	3

Max's mother found that after three days of playing with Max on the swing, having him say "pu" for "push," he was sometimes initiating that request without waiting for the swing to slow

Fig. 3-2 | Teaching Initial Mand with Spoken Prompt

Child: Max   **Teacher:** Mother/father

Target Behavior: Manding for push on swing with verbal prompt.

Behavioral Definition: When asked, "What do you want," with teacher providing spoken prompt ("say push"), Max will echo, "pu."

Description of Program: Help Max sit on swing and give him a few preliminary pushes to start the rhythm of swinging. Teacher stands in front of Max so he can see her and connect motion with her movement. Ensure he is attending to pushes. After a few seconds of pushing and when Max is oriented toward teacher, allow swing to slow. As it slows, if Max shows any agitation or increase in vocalization suggesting he would like more, say to Max, "What do you want?" Immediately provide full spoken prompt, "Say push," but do not make the visual gesture of pushing. If Max makes approximation of word, give the swing several pushes before allowing it to slow again. Repeat the cycle several times and end the session when he fails to show interest in continuing after swing slows.

Use a delayed prompt as needed when Max does not respond to the spoken prompt alone. If Max does not respond with appropriate verbalization after S^D "What do you want," and spoken prompt "Say down. He was also running to the door and waiting for her to go outside with him. It was time to stop offering Max the spoken prompt, "Say push." Beverly did so gradually, by increasing the amount of time between asking, "What do you want?" and giving the model, "Say push." First she waited one second, then two seconds, etc. until she reached a five-second delay of the prompt. After about a week, she was just saying to Max, "What do you want," making the pushing gesture and waiting to push him until he said "pu?" Beverly would look at Max with an expectant expression on her face during the time delay as a subtle prompt that she was waiting for his answer. The technical name for this process of gradually waiting longer and longer to offer the prompt is called "time delay." Figure 3-2 illustrates a program for using a time delay to fade a visual prompt.

push" after 1-second delay, provide visual prompt of pushing gesture. After 3 correct responses with 1-second delay, increase delay of prompt in 1-second intervals until he can respond within 5 seconds without visual prompt. If Max fails to respond after 3 trials at a given level of delay, decrease the delay by 1 second.

S^D for Target Behavior: "What do you want?" with spoken prompt ("Say push").

Consequences: Reinforcement should be inherent in the action of being pushed on swing. Pair this with praise for "nice asking," "good talking." You can say other happy words while you push, such as "This is fun." Be sure he understands words and keep it simple and very enthusiastic

Data Collection: Probe Max's performance on the first three trials of each session. After Max is on the swing and before giving initial push, ask, "What do you want?" with spoken prompt ("Say push") and record his response. Give him a "+" for each correct response and a "-" when he fails to respond. If Max does say an approximation of "push" within specified time, then provide push and repeat probe two more times. If he requests "push" three times in a row with only spoken prompt, it is time to move to next program which will reduce spoken prompt. If Max does not say "push" on the first two probes, simply go on to the next probe. If he fails to respond on the third prompt, you can provide a visual prompt and begin the training cycle.

Another method Beverly might have used to reduce the prompt is called "fading" the prompt. This involves making the length of the prompt briefer and briefer by leaving off the end sounds. For example, "Say push," might have been changed to "Say pu...," and then to "Say...," and then to silence.

Time delay and fading are powerful tools for reducing assistance to a child so gradually that he rarely makes a mistake. Ensuring that he makes few errors and providing a high level of reinforcement help keep him motivated to cooperate and help him enjoy the teaching session. Our goal with children with autism is to have as few errors as possible, an approach called "errorless learning" (Terrace, 1963a,1963b). This is because the fewer errors a child makes, the more he can be reinforced for correct responses and the faster he will learn. In addition, we tend to

---

Fig. 3-3 | Teaching Initial Mand without Prompts

Child: Max   **Teacher:** Mother/father

Target Behavior: Manding for push on swing without prompt.

Behavioral Definition: When asked, "What do you want," Max will say, "Push."

Description of Program: Help Max sit on swing and give him a few preliminary pushes to start the rhythm of swinging. Teacher stands in front of Max so he can see her and connect motion with his movement. Ensure he is attending to pushes. After a few seconds of pushing and when Max is oriented toward teacher, allow swing to slow. As it slows, if Max shows any agitation or increase in sounds, say to Max, "What do you want?" Wait 1 second before providing prompt, "Say push" to allow Max time to respond. If Max responds before prompt with approximation of "push," give the swing several pushes before allowing it to slow again. Repeat the cycle several times, taking care to stop when he ceases to show interest in another push.

If Max does not say "push" after 1 second delay, then provide spoken prompt of "Say push," and when he says, "Push," provide a push. Then repeat trial again, withholding spoken prompt for the specified time. If Max fails to respond after 3 trials at a given level of delay, decrease the delay by 1 second.

repeat errors we have made in the past and the best way to avoid that pattern is to prevent the errors in the first place. For more discussion of errorless learning methods, see the book by Martin and Pear (1983) in the References. Although "errorless learning" is usually not truly without *any* errors, the idea is to keep mistakes to a minimum.

Figure 3-3 illustrates a program for helping Max learn to respond to the question "What do you want?" with neither a visual nor a spoken prompt. Again, this program uses a time delay procedure. You should also note that this program calls for generalization of responding. That means that a child should be exposed to a variety of people and settings when using the mand. For example, the Dunns took Max to the playground, and to the swing set at a neighbor's house to practice the program, and his

After 3 successful trials in a row, increase the amount of time delay before offering verbal prompt. Increase in 1-second increments until reaching 5 seconds with success.

S^D for Target Behavior: "What do you want?"

Consequences: Reinforcement should be inherent in the action of being pushed on swing. Pair this with praise for "nice asking," "good talking." You can say other happy words while you push, such as "This is fun." Be sure words are ones he understands and keep it simple and very enthusiastic

Data Collection: Probe Max's performance on the first 3 trials of each session. After Max is on the swing and before giving initial push, ask "What do you want?" without prompt and record his response. Give him a "+" for each correct response and a "-" when he fails to respond. If Max does say an approximation of "push" within the specified number of seconds, then provide a push and repeat probe 2 more times. If he requests "push" 3 times in a row within 5 seconds without prompting, it is time to move to the next program, which will establish a new mand.

Generalization: After Max shows initial acquisition of this unprompted mand for "push," it should be used in other places such as the park and the school playground. It should also be used by other adults, including his teachers, family members, and family friends. In addition, sometimes push from behind and sometimes from in front of Max.

mother, his father, his grandmother, and one of the neighbors all got involved in pushing him on the swing after Max had shown initial mastery of this program. They also sometimes pushed him from behind and sometimes from in front.

Teaching the Second Mand

Max's enthusiasm for being with his parents and his good response to the time delay for the spoken prompt, "Push," suggested they might expand their teaching efforts. It was time to think about a second mand for Max. Beverly and Wayne decided to add asking for juice, another thing that pleased Max and for which he had a partial label. Like pushes on the swing, sips of juice were something the Dunns could give to Max in small amounts many times. As a result, they could have fairly extended interactions with him around his requests for these items. These

---

Fig. 3-4 | Teaching Second Mand with Full Prompts

Child: Max   **Teacher:** Mother/father

Target Behavior: Manding for juice with verbal ("say juice") and visual (cup) prompts.

Behavioral Definition: When asked, "What do you want," with teacher providing verbal prompt ("say juice") and visual prompt (holding up cup of juice) Max will echo, "ju."

Description of Program: When Max comes in from play outside, have juice container ready on counter. Kneel down in front of him holding a small cup with a little juice and say, "What do you want?" If he makes any gesture toward the cup, immediately provide full spoken prompt, "Say juice." When Max makes approximation of word "juice," give him cup with a few sips of juice. Repeat the cycle several times, taking care to ensure he does not appear to lose interest in juice. Offer him enough to keep him interested, but not so much that he quickly satiates. When he stops gesturing toward cup, end session.

S^D for Target Behavior: "What do you want?" with spoken ("Say juice") and visual (cup of juice) prompts.

two mands, push and juice, were for things that Max could request multiple times without getting tired of them, that he frequently wanted, and that could be quickly consumed, leaving him ready for more.

When Max came into the house, hot and thirsty from running outside, Wayne had a glass of juice on the counter, out of reach, but in sight. He said to his son, "What do you want?" He showed him a small cup of juice while saying, "Say 'juice.'" When Max said "ju," Wayne gave him the sip of juice, a high five, and some words of praise. Over the next several sessions, Wayne gradually stopped giving Max a spoken prompt of "Say juice." Max mastered the word "juice" quicker than he had "push," which was a sign that he was starting to learn how to learn mands. Figure 3-4 details the steps that Max's parents used to teach him his second mand.

Consequences: Reinforcement should be inherent in the action of drinking juice. Pair this with praise for "nice asking" or "good talking."

Other reinforcements such as a high five or clapping for good quality responses should also be used.

Data Collection: Probe Max's performance on the first 3 trials of each session. After Max has come in the house, ask, "What do you want?" with spoken and visual prompts and record his response. Give him a "+" for each correct response and a "-" when he fails to respond. If Max does say an approximation of "juice," then provide small amount and repeat probe 2 more times. If he requests "juice" 3 times in a row with full prompts, it is time to move to next program, which will reduce visual prompt. If he fails to respond on the first 2 probes, just go on to the next. If he fails on the third, proceed with your teaching program as above.

In Figure 3-5 we describe Max's program for eliminating the spoken prompt, "Say juice," while keeping the juice in sight as a visual prompt. After that is accomplished, then the visual prompt is faded as well (See Figure 3-6 on pages 68-69).

Fading The Visual Prompt

Fading the visual prompt of the cup went relatively smoothly for Max. When Max came in hot and sweaty, Beverly would ask him "What do you want?" but would hold the cup of juice behind her back and look at him with an expectant look on her face to see if he would ask for juice. If Max did not say, "juice," she would bring the cup out to show him, and then reinforce him if he asked for juice. She then repeated the question with the juice again behind her back. Max quickly caught on to this and did not need to see the cup to be reminded (prompted) to ask for juice. Instead, he learned that when he came in from outside, he could ask for juice.

Fig. 3-5 | Teaching Initial Mand with Spoken Prompt

Child: Max   **Teacher:** Mother/father

Target Behavior: Manding for juice with visual (cup) prompt only.

Behavioral Definition: When asked, "What do you want," with teacher providing visual prompt (show juice), Max will say, "Juice."

Description of Program: When Max comes in the house from playing outside, have juice container ready on counter. Kneel in front of Max holding the juice. If he reaches toward cup, say, "What do you want?" Allow him 1 second to respond. If he does not, then give spoken prompt, "Say juice." If he repeats word, then give him a sip of juice and immediately repeat, "What do you want?" while showing juice. If Max makes approximation of word before 1 second, give him several sips of juice and repeat cycle. Repeat the cycle several times, making sure he does not appear to become satiated on juice. Stop session when he ceases to reach for juice or ask for it

If Max does not respond after 1-second delay, provide spoken prompt, "Say juice." After 3 correct responses with 1-second delay,

Beverly and Wayne kept in mind that their primary goals at this point were to teach Max to answer the question "What do you want" without a prompt from them, and to keep him highly motivated by providing items in which he had strong interest (i.e., an establishing operation was in effect).

Teaching More Mands

With the first two mands well established and with Max's cooperation during the mand training sessions becoming increasingly reliable, the Dunns moved ahead with helping Max learn to mand for many more attractive items in his environment. For example, he learned to say "Out" to go outside, "Cook" for cookie, and "Up" to ask to be tossed in the air.

Later in training when Max was consistently manding without the physical object in front of him, Beverly and Wayne began to work on teaching Max to ask for things without their asking

---

increase delay of prompt in 1-second intervals until he can respond within 5 seconds without spoken prompt. If Max fails to respond after 3 trials at a given level of delay, decrease the delay by one second.

S^D **for Target behavior:** "What do you want?" without spoken prompt.

Consequences: Reinforcement should be inherent in the action of drinking juice. Pair this with praise for "nice asking" or "good talking." In addition, use other things such as a "high five" or clapping for special quality responses.

Data Collection: Probe Max's performance on the first 3 trials of each session. After Max comes in the house, ask, "What do you want?" while showing him the juice, but without spoken prompt. Record his response. Give him a "+" for each correct response and a "-" when he fails to respond. If Max does say an approximation of "juice" within specified time, then provide juice and repeat probe two more times. If he requests juice 3 times in a row with only a visual prompt, it is time to move to next program which will reduce visual prompt. If he fails to respond on the first 2 probe trials, just go to the next. If he fails on the third probe, return to your teaching program.

him, "What do you want?" They did this by fading out the words in the sentence, "What do you want? The sentence became "What do you…?" and then "What do…" and "What…," and finally they just looked at Max with a questioning expression. This is a good example of the process of fading a prompt. The Dunns could also have used the time delay procedure to accomplish this goal. If they had done that, they would have waited for increasingly longer periods of time before they provided the prompt. See our discussion above about teaching the initial mand for a longer description of using a time delay.

As Max gained some functional language to request things he wanted, and as his interactions with the adults in his life grew more reinforcing, he became a more responsive, coopera-

---

Fig. 3-6 | Teaching Second Mand without Prompts

Child: Max   **Teacher:** Mother/father

Target Behavior: Manding for juice without prompts.

Behavioral Definition: When asked, "What do you want," without teacher providing prompts, Max will say, "juice."

Description of Program: When Max comes in the house from playing outside, have juice container ready, but out of his sight. Kneel in front of Max, and, holding the juice behind your back say, "What do you want?" Allow him 1 second to respond. If he does not, then show him the juice. If he says "juice" after visual prompt, give him a sip of juice and immediately repeat cycle saying, "What do you want?" without showing juice. If Max does make approximation of word before 1 second, give him a sip of juice and repeat cycle. Repeat the cycle several times, making sure he does not appear to become satiated on juice. End session when he stops requesting juice or reaching for it.

If Max does not respond after 1-second delay, provide visual prompt. After 3 correct responses with 1-second pause, increase delay of prompt in 1-second intervals until he can respond within 5 seconds without visual prompt. If Max fails to respond after 3 trials at a given level of delay, decrease the delay by 1 second.

tive child who had fewer tantrums. This gave the family and his school the opportunity to address his language and other skills much more intensively. For example, Beverly and Wayne broadened the kinds of requests they were making of Max. In the morning when Max said, "Want juice," Beverly might respond, "First put on shirt, and then I'll give you juice." Max would hold up his arms for his mother to slip the shirt over his head. What had once been a source of a tantrum each morning when he was getting dressed quickly became routine good behavior. Max's parents expanded that cooperation into having Max begin to dress himself with small rewards along the way. In school, his teacher was using the things Max manded for to teach him more advanced language and other important skills.

S^D for Target behavior: "What do you want?"

Consequences: Reinforcement should be inherent in the action of drinking juice. Pair this with praise for "nice asking" or "good talking." In addition, use other things such as a "high five" or clapping for special quality responses.

Data Collection: Probe Max's performance on the first 3 trials of each session. After Max comes in the house ask, "What do you want" without prompt and record his response. Give him a "+" for each correct response and a "-" when he fails to respond. If Max does say an approximation of "juice" within specified time, then provide juice and repeat probe 2 more times. If he requests juice 3 times in a row within 5 seconds of S^D, it is time to move to next program which will ensure generalized responding to significant others.

Generalization: After Max shows initial acquisition of this unprompted mand for "juice," it should be used in other places such as the backyard, in school at lunch time, and during family meals. It should be used for different juices and with different cups and glasses. The program should also be used by other adults, including his teachers, family members, and friends. In addition, the adults should be in different physical relationships to Max such as both standing, both seated, next to the refrigerator, at the kitchen table, etc.

Troubleshooting

Here are answers to some of the common questions that arise about teaching manding:

What to Do about Tantrums? That is, what if your child refuses to make a request for a desired item but instead has a tantrum? The answer involves two components. First, in order to minimize the risk of tantrums, make sure that the first response you are teaching your child is something he can do. For example, make sure that he is able to make a certain sound before requiring that as a response. If spoken words or sounds are more difficult or less consistent, then be sure to choose a response you can help your child make, like a manual sign or the use of a picture. Also, be sure that you do not increase the level of demand too sharply so that the response becomes difficult for your child. Second, if he does have a tantrum, do not give him the item, or else you will be reinforcing tantrum behavior rather than appropriate manding. There are many ways to deal with tantrums and you and your child's teacher or consultant should have a plan for how to address the behavior when it does occur.

Do You Have to Respond to Every Mand? Parents also wonder if they must do as their child wishes each time he makes a mand. To the extent it is possible, it is important to respond to every spontaneous mand. However, life is full of complexity, and if you are changing the baby when your child mands for juice, you may not be able to respond immediately. The best thing to do then is what you would do with any child who asks for something and must wait. That is, ask your child to wait and then provide the juice as soon as you can. Perhaps you can distract him with some other handy item. Don't forget that if he has a tantrum, at that point you can't calm him down by giving him the juice. Follow your plan for dealing with tantrums. Sometimes it is not possible to give a child the exact thing he wants. For example, he mands for orange juice and you only have apple juice. Offer the alternative. If he takes it, you are in luck. If he doesn't, suggest another activity to engage him, but again, if he tantrums, you must deal firmly with that behavior (and try to go shopping for orange juice as soon as you can!)

Who Should Respond to Your Child's Mands? If your child is to learn to use his requests with people beyond you, it is important that other people become involved in responding to his mands. His siblings, grandparents, aunts, and uncles should all become part of the teaching team. If a younger sibling is too small to respond or his grandfather doesn't want to be bothered, your child will learn not to make requests of them.

What If Your Child Doesn't Understand Your Words? Some children with autism have a very limited ability to either express themselves or understand what other people are saying. Mand training, like other aspects of language learning, may go more slowly for them. However, you will still want to start your teaching with establishing compliance and teaching basic mands. By carefully arranging the environment and using visual cues and prompts, the expectations can often be made clearer for your child. See the book by Sundberg and Partington (1998) for help in teaching language to children with autism who have little, if any, initial language.

Summary

Typically developing children learn very early to ask for things they want, first with gestures and then with words. For many children with autism, learning to make those requests is much more daunting. The goal of mand training is to teach children to request items or experiences that are reinforcing. When a child can make those requests, we use those mands as an opportunity to ask a child to do a little work for us. Mand training is also the foundation for many other language functions, including labeling (tacting), receptive identification, and conversation (intraverbals). Once your child has learned to mand, you can use it as a routine part of interactions with him.

References

Bondy, A. & Frost, L. (2002). *A Picture's Worth: PECS and Other Visual Communication Strategies in Autism.* Bethesda, MD: Woodbine House.

Martin, G. & Pear, J. (1983). *Behavior Modification: What It Is and How to Do It.* Englewood Cliffs, NJ: Prentice Hall.

Michael, J. (1982). Distinguishing between discriminative and motivational functions of stimuli. *Journal of the Experimental Analysis of Behavior*, 32, 149-155.

Skinner, B.F. (1957). *Verbal Behavior.* Englewood Cliffs, NJ: Prentice Hall.

Sundberg, M. L. & Partington, J. W. (1998). *Teaching Language to Children with Autism or Other Developmental Disabilities.* Pleasant Hill, CA: Behavior Analysts, Inc.

Terrace, H. S. (1963A). Discrimination learning with and without "errors." *Journal of Experimental Analysis of Behavior,* 6, 1-27.

Terrace, H. S. (1963B). Errorless transfer of a discrimination across two continua. *Journal of Experimental Analysis of Behavior,* 6, 223-232.

4 | Making Choices: "I Prefer That"

The Ramirez Family

At eleven years of age, Maria Ramirez was becoming a young woman. Although she took little note of her appearance, Maria was in transition from girl to teenager. Her mother, Rosa, took pride in her daughter's achievements, but also knew a lot of hard work lay ahead. Maria's autism made every step of learning more challenging than it was for most children. In spite of that, she was a good girl who was a big help around the house and who had a wonderful sense of humor. Maria was an only child and her father, Hector, had died while she was baby, so Maria and Rosa spent a great deal of time together.

At age three, Maria had been enrolled in an early intervention program for children with autism. Although she made good progress there, she continued to need considerable support as she progressed through school. Maria had mild mental retardation as well as autism and needed help learning the full array of self-help and prevocational skills.

From early childhood, Rosa has worked to teach Maria to make choices. When Maria was a little girl, Rosa would show her several different items and ask which one she wanted to work for. For example, she might offer her a cracker, a small cup of juice, or a toy car and ask her which one she wanted. Later, when they were working on dressing, Rosa would present choices about which clothing Maria wanted to wear to school and what she wanted for breakfast. As a result, Maria learned early how to make some choices for herself.

In school, Maria learned to arrange her photographic activity schedule in the order she wanted to follow. For example, each morn-

ing she was given cards with pictures of the four different teaching programs she would be doing and the four short break activities she could do. Maria was encouraged to arrange these tasks in the order she wanted to complete them, with each work session followed by one break. Rosa used a similar schedule with Maria when she got home from school. Initially Mrs. Ramirez arranged the pictures and Maria followed the schedule. Then Maria learned to arrange the schedule on her own. Some days she would have her snack first, and other days she would do her homework, watch a video, and have her snack before she helped make dinner. Most recently, Maria has learned to both select the activities she plans to do, and then write them down in the order she wants to follow.

Being allowed to make her own choices throughout the day gives Maria some control over what happens to her and seems to give her a sense of "ownership" when she makes up her schedule.

Discussion

Many people with autism, like most of the rest of us, seem to prefer to make their own choices. It is interesting to think about how many choices we do make every day. The alarm wakes us. Hit the snooze button or get up right away? A choice. We put on our sweats (which color today?) and head out the door for a run. Which way to go today? Back for a shower, but it could have been a bath if we wanted. Pick out the clothing for the day. Which color? Which style? Downstairs to breakfast. Toast? Cereal? Eggs? Juice? Coffee or tea? And so it goes until we decide to go bed. Scores of small choices all day, and, of course, big ones also. Where to go on vacation? Which car to buy? Which person to marry? We value our freedom of choice, and many of us would get pretty cranky if it were taken away. People have fought revolutions over lack of choice in the control of their government.

Even people of limited cognitive ability or very young children who cannot understand that pictures represent objects can make some choices by being presented with the actual items. For example, a child might be shown a blue shirt and a red shirt and asked to select the one she wants to wear. All of the people with autism with whom we have worked have learned to make at least basic choices and many have developed the ability to make complex choices. A person's cognitive skills may determine the kinds of choice she can make, but there are few people who cannot learn to make some choices.

On both ethical and pragmatic grounds, there is good reason to advocate for giving people with autism as much choice as they can safely manage. People who use the principles of Applied Behavior Analysis to teach are called upon to treat their child, student, or adult learner with dignity. Part of that respectful stance is encouraging the individual to make his or her own choices within broad guidelines that ensure safety and respect for other people. People with autism are entitled to make their own choices, but they need help in learning to understand the concept of choice and being able to initiate choices.

There are studies showing the benefits of making choices in different contexts. For example, workers with disabilities who were allowed to select the tools they would use were found to consistently select the tools that would allow them to function more independently, with less job coach support (Reid, Parsons, Green & Browning, 2001). Similarly, students with autism and other serious disorders exhibit fewer problem behaviors when allowed to choose activities (e.g., Dyer, Dunlap & Winterling, 1990; Vaughn & Horner, 1997).

How Do You Teach Choice Making?

We have already discussed some of the elements of choice making. In Chapter 2, we described the process of identifying a reinforcer for a person with autism. Although some people's preferences for reinforcers may be very clear, for others, it may be important to do an assessment and observe them to see which items attract their attention. In addition, as you know from our discussion of Establishing Operations (EOs) in Chapter 2, prefer- ences are often in a state of change. For instance, when you place two items, a cracker and a stacking toy, on the table and your child typically picks up the cracker, she has made a choice, at least for that moment. After she eats the cracker, her preferences may shift and she may not want another or she may tire of the stacking toy and want to play with something else.

Another skill related to choice making, mand training, is described in Chapter 3. When a child learns to mand, she can make spontaneous requests for the items or events that she wants. Manding is a powerful tool because the learner has developed the ability to ask for things that are out of sight and to request things at times when you may not be asking her what she wants. You do not have to be a mind reader and she does not have to have a tantrum in a futile effort to communicate her desires.

Choice making can go beyond naming simple reinforcers, to include arranging work schedules, selecting clothing, planning meals, and deciding which video to watch. The purpose of the present chapter is to describe some of the methods you can use to teach the skills needed for these more complex choices. The range of life activities that provide opportunities for choice make it clear that this is a skill that is meaningful for mature adults as well as for children and adolescents.

We can only give a few examples about specific choices in the space of this chapter and we have selected our examples with the hope that you will be able to transfer the same proce- dures to the many other choice points of the day. Thus, we focus below on the steps for helping a child learn to select clothing because it is a very useful skill for any child, can be narrowed to two items, and eventually will make your day easier. However, the same fundamental idea applies to making choices about foods, activities, toys, and chores.

If your adult child has not learned to make choices, you can use the methods we describe here to teach her, although you will likely offer her different items to choose from than you would offer a younger child. Children who learned to make simple choices when they were very young will also need ongoing help to support their learning to expand their choice making. We saw this in the case of Maria Ramirez, who advanced from choosing her reinforcers to selecting clothing to planning her work schedule. Undoubtedly, she will continue to develop even more complex work and leisure skills as she matures.

What to Wear?

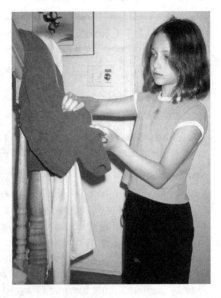

We stand in front of the closet each morning. Decisions …decisions. We select the things we want to wear and check ourselves out in the mirror. Does that color work OK? Is the collar straight? And so forth. It is important for people with autism, too, to learn to make choices of clothing and to select colors that go together and clothing that matches the weather and event.

For the young child, clothing choices can be made from two different selections that parents lay out for them. For example, a blue t-shirt and a yellow t-shirt may be offered and then a choice of shorts and socks to make a complete outfit. As children get older, they can make their own choices from the array of socks, t-shirts, shorts, and other clothing in their dresser drawers.

An example of a basic clothing choice program is shown in Figure 4-1 on the next page. (If you need help understanding the vocabulary on that form, see the section called "Elements of Teaching Programs" in Chapter 3 where we discuss those terms.) Little Tawana, who was forty months old, learned to select all her own clothing when her father followed this program at home. Because her mother worked the night shift as a nurse, Tawana's father dressed her each morning and taught her to make these choices. The program is typical of ones we suggest to parents of preschool-aged children at our Center, and is designed to allow a child to make a series of choices to create a coordinated outfit. Parents retain sufficient control to ensure that their child is dressed appropriately for the weather conditions and the event, and within those broad parameters the child has a choice as well. Notice that

---

Fig. 4-1 | Choosing Clothing

Child: Tawana   **Teacher:** Parents

Target Behavior: Tawana will choose between two different items of clothing that differ in color or style.

Behavioral Definition: When offered a choice of two items of clothing that differ in color or style, Tawana will point to the one she prefers.

Description of Program: When Tawana is getting dressed in the morning, she will be offered a choice between two t-shirts or blouses that differ in color or style and be told, "Choose a shirt." She is to respond by pointing to the one she wants. In the early stage of the program, use one shirt that she very much likes and another that is not of great interest to her. She will put on the shirt she selected.

In the first stage of teaching, if Tawana fails to respond, prompt her by gently guiding her hand toward the preferred shirt. As she begins to assume some initiative in pointing to the shirt, fade your physical prompt. If she fails to respond after several seconds of your pointing, try moving the preferred shirt closer to her. When Tawana is consistently pointing to one shirt or another and accepting it to put on, introduce choice for her socks, shorts, pants, or skirt. It is important that Tawana wear the item she selects.

After Tawana has learned to choose between two items where one is clearly preferred, you can allow her to make choices among several different shorts, skirts, etc. If she consistently chooses only one specific item, remove that from the array on some days to encourage her to make other choices.

When she can select the item she wants from an array that you select for her, the next step will be to allow her to remove items from

the program outlines the process of going from selecting between two pieces of clothing, one of which is known to be a favorite of the child's, to several pieces of clothing to make an entire outfit. Once the child can make choices between items the parents have selected, she will move on to making choices from a broader array of clothing in her dresser and her closet.

Some children may get confused about the number of items to select, and, for example, take several shirts. If your child does that, you might consider having her use a photographic activity

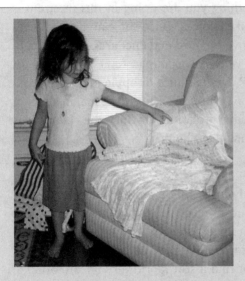

a drawer or from her closet. If need be, you can limit the number of items that are visible so she learns to generalize the skill to the location where her clothing is stored. Ultimately, you will want to have the full array of clothing present.

S^D for Task: The parent will say to Tawana, "Time to get dressed. Choose," and hold up the two items.

Consequences: Praise Tawana's choice, saying "Good choice. That is pretty!" or "I like that color," etc. Then allow her to wear the item she selects and perhaps tell her again how good she looks when she puts it on.

Data Collection: Record a "+" if Tawana points to an item of clothing. If she needs prompts, score this as "-." Make a note also if she selects the same item repeatedly, as you will want to vary her choices to avoid that lack of variation.

Generalization: Tawana should learn to make choices of many different items of clothing, to make her choices at the dresser and closet. and to make choices for both of her parents, as well as for other adults who might care for her.

schedule in which each page depicts one item of clothing such as underwear, socks, shirt, pants, and shoes (McClannahan & Krantz, 1999). If she can read, this could be a written checklist.

If your child has problems matching colors, you can organize her clothing by units with the colors that mix well bundled together so she selects a set of items. You could also focus on buying her clothing that can be readily intermixed. For example, if you buy only solid-colored blue and black slacks, many shirts with different patterns could be matched with them.

Remember, the key thing you are doing in this program is teaching your child to make choices. Once she can make choices in this context you can move forward and encourage choice making for other contexts as well. For example, tuna fish or peanut butter and jelly for lunch? Orange juice or apple juice for breakfast? Roller blading or doing a puzzle? The choice making can, of course, be linked to language programs in which the child learns to mand for (request) items that she prefers.

Troubleshooting

Although we typically insist that a child stay with a choice so that she learns the concept of choice, there are some exceptions. Some children with autism have sensory issues related to clothing or food. For example, they may be bothered by the tag on the back of the shirt or find a stiff fabric very uncomfortable. Similarly, some foods may be too soft, crunchy, salty, etc. for a particular child. We try to be sensitive to those issues and not insist that a child wear something that is not comfortable or eat a food that is unpleasant. We think it is fine to cut the tags off a shirt, only buy items the child will like, and remove clothing from the wardrobe if she finds it aversive. If a child selects a new piece of clothing and finds it is uncomfortable once she tries it on, we would not ordinarily insist that she wear it, even though it was her choice. To avoid this problem when first teaching choices, use only familiar items that your child wears willingly (or, in the case of foods, has eaten in the past).

Another problem that sometimes arises is when a child has very rigid choices. For example, she will only wear a single shirt. If that is the case, you should not use shirts to teach the concept of choice, and you will need to address increasing her range of acceptable shirts before moving on to making choices of shirts. Your child's teacher or consultant should be able to help you create a teaching program to encourage your child to tolerate less preferred items for longer periods of time. While you are doing that, you can work on making choices of other things, such as games to play or desserts to make.

Arranging Schedules for Work and Play

Many older children and adults with autism spectrum disorders can benefit from learning to arrange their daily schedules and deciding on the order of events, to the extent that such choices are feasible. The school-aged child can start by arranging her schedule of activities when she comes home from school, as we saw in the case of Maria Ramirez that opened this chapter. Maria had several tasks to do when she got home, including changing into her play clothes, getting her own snack, taking out the trash, feeding the cat, and setting the table. She also was allowed to watch 30 minutes of television or videos in the afternoon, to play computer games for 30 minutes, and to spend another 30 minutes in an activity of her choosing. Initially, her mother, Rosa, had taken pictures of Maria doing these tasks or of the items needed for the activities, such as a can of cat food or the VCR. Then she taught Maria how to organize the tasks herself. Maria was allowed to arrange these in any order she wished, except that she had to change her clothes when she first came in.

Overview of Activity Schedules

Mrs. Ramirez had introduced a photographic activity schedule early in Maria's education and this was the device she used to

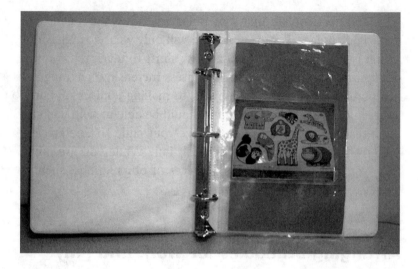

teach her daughter to set her own after-school schedule. Psychologists Lynn McClannahan and Patricia Krantz (1999) have written a wonderful book entitled *Activity Schedules for Children with Autism* on teaching children to follow activity schedules, and we will not go into the basics in great detail here. We will give a brief overview of how activity schedules work and then focus on ways to teach older children and young adults with autism to make their own activity schedules.

The typical photographic activity schedule consists of a three-ring binder that has pictures of one or more activities the child needs to do, as well as one or more reinforcers she enjoys. The photos are laminated for durability, and mounted on pages with Velcro backing. Initially, the child's schedule may consist of a single photograph of an activity she needs to complete on the first page, followed by a photograph of the reward she will receive for doing the task on the next page. The child learns to open the binder, look at the photo of the activity she must do, complete that activity, turn the page and access the reinforcer pictured on that page.

As a child, Maria learned to follow page by page the activities in her photographic activity schedule. Her first book consisted of two pictures. One was of a puzzle and the second was of a small snack. She learned to do the puzzle and then get the snack from a nearby shelf. Gradually, her mother added more activities and then she began to change the order so that Maria did not fall into a rote pattern of doing everything the same way each day. Maria learned to use her book independently and skillfully.

As McClannahan and Krantz point out, to use this kind of schedule, the child needs to learn that the photos represent objects or activities. If you have never used this kind of schedule, you will want to consult someone who has experience in their use or read a book such as the one by McClannahan and Krantz that will walk you through the necessary steps.

Being able to make choices is not essential to the first stages of a photographic activity schedule. A parent or teacher can assemble the pages in a sequence they determine. However, as your child matures, you will want her to make her own choices. This means you should be working on choice making as a separate activity, which you will then blend into the planning of a schedule. When Maria was younger and had learned to follow a simple activity schedule, her mother taught her to choose between pictures of two or more potential reinforcers to select the one she preferred and to choose between two or more pictures of enjoyable activities to do the one she wanted to do. These were then inserted into the schedule. Maria understood that the pictures represented her options, and the picture she selected determined the item she received. Maria was very skillful at making those choices. If your child cannot make those kinds of basic choices, you should consult the book by McClannahan and Krantz (1999) for help in teaching her those skills.

Once children learn to read and write, they often transition from using a photographic activity schedule to a written schedule—because it's more efficient and age appropriate. Like Maria, they shift from using photos to using cards with the names of the activities written on them. Maria's mother first included written labels with the pictures and then the gradually faded out the pictures, so only the words remained. Maria also learned to copy the order of the activities from words on the cards to a paper list and to check off the items as she completed them. As she taught these skills to Maria, Mrs. Ramirez took care to deliver her prompts when standing behind Maria and to fade the prompts as soon as she could so that Maria did not become dependent on her mother's prompts.

Teaching Your Child to Make Her Own Activity Schedule

It is a major developmental advance when a person is ready to create her own schedules. Being able to plan your own day contributes greatly to maximizing independence. Many people on the spectrum of autism can learn this skill, and, as a result, need less supervision. In addition, they experience the pleasure that comes with making many choices for themselves each day.

As we noted earlier in this chapter, we tend to take choice making and schedule planning for granted in our own lives, and may not recognize how much we value it until it is taken away. There is no reason to think people with autism do not derive similar pleasure from having whatever control is feasible over their own lives. To exercise that freedom, they need to learn the skills for organizing their day and choosing among activities to ensure that both essential and optional activities find their place in the schedule. Should they have unlimited choice? None of us do. Some things *must* be done and sometimes they must be done at a specific time. Should people with autism have as many choices as possible? The rest of us do!

Table 4-1 | Maria's Optional Work Choices

[Select two]

◆ Set table	◆ Make salad
◆ Make dessert	◆ Empty trash cans
◆ Empty dishwasher	◆ Fold laundry
◆ Return recycling can to garage	◆ Scrub toilet
	◆ Clean litter box

In order to teach Maria to transition from a schedule planned by her mother to one that was of her own choosing, Mrs. Ramirez followed the instructions in McClannahan and Krantz's book. Mrs. Ramirez used a new three-ring notebook and put pictures of her choices of after-school activities on the front and back covers with Velcro. Having them there allowed Maria to scan her options, pull them off the Velcro on the cover, and stick them on the Velcro of the page in the book. Initially she had to prompt her daughter to select a first activity from the front cover, put it on a page in the notebook, do that activity, and then select a new photo, and so on.

With that solid base of skills established, Rosa Ramirez was ready to teach Maria to decide for herself the order in which she wanted to do her after-school work and recreational activities. Because Maria had used schedules of various kinds for many years, she was very fluent in following them and did not need help in understanding the basic idea of a schedule nor how to move from one item to the next. There were specific activities that Mrs. Ramirez wanted Maria to do each day when she got home and there were other things that were up to Maria to choose among. Mrs. Ramirez did not care how Maria ordered the tasks so long as they were all done before dinner.

As illustrated in Figure 4-2 on the next page, Maria's current schedule focuses on her selecting the items and the order in which she does her afternoon work and recreational activities. Now that

---

Table 4-2 | Maria's Optional Recreation Activities

[If she completes one early, she may select another for the remaining time.]

◆ Look at teen magazine	◆ Watch TV
◆ Watch video or DVD	◆ Eat snack
◆ Do puzzle	◆ Talk to Mom
◆ Do art project	◆ Roller blade in driveway
◆ Call Grandma and Grandpa	◆ Listen to music
◆ Just relax!	

she can read, Maria no longer needs photographs, but has two sets of written items to choose from. Her work activities are written on a set of blue cards, and her recreational activities are on a set of white cards. (See Tables 4-1 and 4-2 on the previous pages.) Maria knows that there are two required items: homework and feeding the cat. Each day Maria selects two additional work activities beyond the required ones and three recreational activities.

When Maria comes home in the afternoon, she greets her mother, talks for a few minutes, and then goes to her room to change her clothes. When she comes back to the kitchen, Mrs. Ramirez says, "Plan your schedule." At that point, Maria gets her box of 3x5 cards with the different tasks written on them, lays them out in front of her, selects the ones she is going to do, and writes them on her schedule sheet. She then does the tasks in the

Fig. 4-2 | Making Choices of Work and Play at Home

Child: Maria   **Teacher:** Mother

Target Behavior: Select and order after-school activities.

Behavioral Definition: Maria will remove two free choice work tasks, three recreational tasks, and the two required work tasks from her card box, lay them out on the table in front of her, put them in the order she wishes to follow, and write them on her schedule sheet. She will follow this order to complete the activities.

Description of Program: When Maria comes home from school, greets her mother, changes her clothes, and returns to the kitchen, Mrs. R. will say, "Plan your schedule," and Maria will go to her file box and remove 7 cards (2 required tasks, 2 chosen tasks, and 3 recreational tasks). She will lay them all out in front of her. She will then write them on her schedule sheet in the order she wishes to follow and begin the schedule. (Note: it may help to color code the cards and dividers. For example, yellow might be required work, blue optional work, and red leisure activities.)

The box of tasks should have 3 major dividers, one for "Required Work" with two 3x5 cards labeled "homework" and "feed cat," another for "Work Choices" with cards labeling the full range of order listed and checks off each item as she completes it. This complex set of behaviors is built on many years of teaching Maria to make choices and to follow schedules. The payoff for all that work is not only that Maria is quite self-sufficient for many hours, but also that Mrs. Ramirez has time for her own work with only periodic checks to ensure Maria is doing her work and to give her daughter well-deserved praise.

Behavioral Issues and Choice Making

Maria Ramirez is a gentle child who rarely poses problems for her mother. For her, learning to make choices was most useful in helping her become more independent. For other individuals with autism spectrum disorders, making choices can be helpful

---

optional work tasks, and a third divider for "Recreation Choices." (See list of work and recreation choices.)

Maria has mastered previous programs for creating schedules and this program is one that requires her to generalize her selection and schedule following skills to some new activities.

Mrs. R can add new optional work tasks and recreation tasks and Maria may also suggest new items to add.

S^D for Task: "Plan your schedule."

Consequences: Periodically during the afternoon Mrs. R. can compliment Maria on how well she is working. There are also recreation programs built into the schedule.

Data Collection: Record a "+" or "-" for each of the following: 1) choosing the activities, 2) putting activities in order, 3) completing each activity. Make note also of Maria's choices, and if she does not have some variation, consider removing some often-selected cards and replacing them with others to ensure she does not become too rigid in her choices. Be sure to stay behind Maria and out of sight when collecting data or if she needs any prompts.

Generalization: This program is designed to facilitate generalization of a skill learned in previous programs.

A choice board used for an older adolescent.

in dealing with serious behavior management problems. For some people, the simple act of making choices serves to reduce behavior problems. The opportunity to obtain the things they want by choosing among items becomes more motivating than does their challenging behavior.

Sarah was among the more challenging clients in our adult program. She had frequent tantrums that often included self-injury. She would slap her face with her open hand and sometimes with a closed fist. These behaviors were worrisome to the staff and to the aunt and uncle who were caring for Sarah after the death of her parents some years earlier.

When she was not involved in tantrums and self-injury, Sarah was capable of doing a variety of tasks, including using a copier, operating a paper folder, and stuffing envelopes. She also knew how to prepare simple meals, dress herself, and enjoyed several recreational activities such as bowling and going to the mall.

Our first step in addressing Sarah's behavior was to do an evaluation called a functional assessment. This assessment was used to determine what factors triggered Sarah's tantrums. First we defined the target behaviors and then we watched her at work and tried to identify some environmental events that might be the antecedents (precursors) to her tantrums. That is, we watched to see what happened just before the tantrum. We also collected data on what happened just after the behavior (the consequences). This assessment revealed that making work demands on Sarah was most likely to trigger the tantrums. (A full description of the process of functional assessment is beyond the scope of this book. For more information about functional assessments, see the book *Functional Assessment and Program Development for Problem Behavior* by R.E. O'Neill and his colleagues (1997), which describes the process in detail.

Once we identified the antecedents (triggers) of Sarah's tantrums, we put a comprehensive program in place to address the behaviors. One component of this program was an opportunity for Sarah to select her work activities and her break time activities each morning and afternoon. Figure 4-3 on the next page illustrates the details of this program. Among her work choices were running the copier, using the paper folding machine, applying labels to envelopes, and putting the envelopes in zip code order before they were taken to the post office. Her break time activities included working on a puzzle, making jewelry, going for a walk, and playing Frisbee.

Because Sarah had already learned how to use a picture schedule for selecting and ordering recreational activities, we did not have to teach her basic choice making, but only applied this to a broader portion of her day at the Center.

We have data on Sarah's tantrums during three months before the choice program was put into effect and for four months after choice was added to her program. During the pre-choice period, Sarah's tantrums showed a steady increase each month, going from less then 1 episode a week to 2 episodes a week, and then 7 or 8 a week. It was clearly time to try something new and that is when we introduced choice into Sarah's full day at the Center. The impact on tantrums was immediate with a decline to less than 1 episode a week over the next 4 months. Although the clinical nature of the results did not allow us to do the kind of controlled experiment that would prove it was choice making which influenced Sarah's behavior, the results do support the idea that choice making may be helpful for some clients with significant behavior problems. We have seen choice making improve the behavior of a number of people with autism including children, adolescents, and adults.

Fig. 4-3 | Using Choice Making to Reduce Tantrums with Self-Injury

Client: Sarah   **Coach:** Emily

Target Behaviors: 1) Select and order work & recreational activities; 2) Reduction of tantrums with self-injury.

Behavioral Definitions: 1) Choose photos of work and recreational activities from bulletin board and place on Schedule Sheet.
2) Tantrums are defined as screaming, shouting "NO," stamping her feet, or forcefully pulling away from the individual making a request.
3) Self-injury is defined as any episode in which Sarah uses her open hand or closed fist to strike any part of her body. See details on program sheet for tantrums with self-injury.

Description of Program: Sarah will choose from a varied assortment of work and recreational activities represented with digital photos on a bulletin board in the lounge. The photos are removed by Sarah from the board upon selection and placed on her schedule board. Activities will end after a period of 5 to15 minutes, at which time the coach will inform Sarah that it is time to choose another activity. Upon initial implementation, a 50% ratio of vocational/academic activities of daily living tasks to recreational (sports/music/walks) activities will be maintained on the bulletin board, using

Choice Making at School

We integrate choice making as fully as we can into the days of our students with autism spectrum disorders, no matter what their age. At school, however, children need to learn that there are times when they can choose and times when they must follow someone else's schedule. For example, the entire group may be going out to lunch, working on math, or reading. Our goal for our students is not for them to have total control over all they do, but to make those choices that are fitting. That is something that everyone in our society needs to understand. We do not have full control over all we do each day.

When we are working on teaching choice making in class, we go out of our way to offer many opportunities for a child to

midday replacement of all the photos. The ratio of task to recreation will be changed (decreasing recreational options) by one photo with each 25% decrease in total frequency of self-injury.

Sarah has previously mastered choice making and scheduling and there should be minimal need for prompts. Use verbal and gestural prompts as needed, and fade.

If tantrums and/or self-injurious behavior occurs, follow procedures in program sheet for managing these behaviors.

S^D for Task: The Coach will say to Sarah, "Time to make up your schedule. Choose."

Consequences: Reinforcement should be inherent in the action of Sarah's selecting her preferred activities. Pair this with praise such as "Great choices," or "You really did a good job with your schedule," or "____ is fun." High fives and pats on the back can also be used.

Data Collection: Record a "+" for each photo Sarah independently selects and puts in order on her sheet. Record a "-" if she needs prompts for a selection. See the existing protocol on self-injurious behavior for recording this behavior. Be sure to prompt from behind.

Generalization: Periodically add new photos as Sarah's activities change and to maintain her interest. This program will be transferred to home when Sarah's response is consistent at the Center and we have determined that her tantrums with self-injury have decreased.

learn the skill. After she learns the skill, she must also learn to discriminate those times when she has a choice from those times when she must follow someone else's plan. Knowing what lies ahead and when they can and cannot make choices seems to be helpful to many people with autism for whom ambiguity and unexpected events can be stressful.

There are many ways to inject choice into the school day. For example, if a teacher wishes to accomplish four different programs with a student, she may invite her to put these in the order she wishes to follow. In addition, a student can select the items she wants to eat in the school cafeteria, or eat a lunch that she assembled while at home. She may have several different activities she can do during math or reading time, choose from among a variety of playground activities, decide on her own book in the library, and select her preferred playmate for a game or learning partner in the classroom. Once we become alert to encouraging choices, it becomes evident just how many there can be over the course of the day.

Summary

The benefits of learning to make choices are not limited to any age group or to individuals of any particular level of intelligence or placement on the autism spectrum. Whether your child is a teenager with autistic disorder who has behavior problems, a preschool child with Asperger's disorder, or an adult with autistic disorder and mental retardation, he or she can learn to make choices and enjoy the pleasure that control typically brings. The kinds of choices and degree of independence that an individual ultimately achieves will certainly vary with her skills, but almost everyone with autism can learn to assert herself and make choices of some important things such as food, clothing, or recreational or work activities. Being able to make requests (mand) and to follow a schedule are two sets of skills that play an important role in many kinds of choice making.

References

Dyer, K., Dunlap, G., & Winterling, V. (1990). Effects of choice making on the serious problem behaviors of students with severe handicaps. *Journal of Applied Behavior Analysis,* 23, 515-24.

McClannahan, L. E., & Krantz, P. J. (1999). *Activity Schedules for Children with Autism: Teaching Independent Behavior.* Bethesda, MD: Woodbine House.

O'Neill, R. E., Horner, R. H., Albin, R. W., Sprague, J. R., Storey, K. & Newton, J. S. (1997). *Functional Assessment and Program Development for Problem Behavior: A Practical Handbook.* Pacific Grove, CA: Brooks/Cole Publishing Co.

Reid, D. H., Parsons, M. B., Green, C. W., & Browning, L. B. (2001). Increasing one aspect of self-determination among adults with severe multiple disabilities in supported work. *Journal of Applied Behavior Analysis,* 34, 341-44.

Vaughn, B. J., & Horner, R. H. (1997). Identifying instructional tasks that occasion problem behaviors and assessing the effects of student versus teacher choice among these tasks. *Journal of Applied Behavior Analysis,* 30, 299-312.

5 | Token Systems: "I'll Buy That"

The Yang Family

Jeremy Yang was learning to be a big help around the house. Every morning he carried the garbage out to the trashcan before he left for school and each afternoon he set the table for dinner, cleared the dishes after dinner, and put them in the dishwasher. His parents were determined that Jeremy would be a part of family life in spite of his autism, and in a household with four other children, Jeremy's contribution was important.

When Jeremy was very young and first learning to set the table, Mrs. Yang put placemats with a picture of each utensil on the table. Jeremy learned to match the spoon, knife, and so forth to the outline on the placemat. At first he was just putting down the spoons, then spoons and forks, and so on, until after about three months, he was laying out the place setting for each person.

When Jeremy started learning to put out the utensils, Mrs. Yang would praise him and give him a penny for each spoon that he did correctly. Then he could exchange the pennies for a small treat when he had finished with the spoons. Next, she withheld the penny until he had put down both the spoon and the fork. Then, when he could do those two, he had to do the spoon, fork, and knife to earn his penny. Finally, he was receiving a penny for each place setting. Although his teacher had been using a simple token system for Jeremy for several months, this was the first time Mrs. Yang had used one at home and she was pleased with the results.

In his introduction to token systems at school and at home, Jeremy learned that the pennies he received for doing good work *were quickly exchanged for things he really wanted, such as sips of soda, potato chips, or access to a favorite toy. The pennies, which had no initial interest for Jeremy, came to have value because they were linked to the things he did like. This link became a powerful tool for his parents and teachers over the years because using tokens enabled Jeremy to work for longer-term goals, rather than receiving only immediate rewards.*

As Jeremy grew older, he no longer needed to receive pennies; simple marks (points) on a piece of paper came to serve as reinforcement instead. Once he was integrated into a regular education class in his local school, Jeremy had homework to do each night. If he did his homework neatly and completed all of his assignments within a specified amount of time, he earned points that were recorded on a sheet of paper above his desk. At the end of the week, if he had enough points, he could cash them in for a variety of special events over the weekend, including going to a movie, playing ball with his father, or working on his hobby with his mother.

Discussion

Token systems can be a powerful tool for increasing the motivation of some children with autism spectrum disorders. Once they grasp the idea that pennies, poker chips, or marks on a piece of paper can be exchanged for things they want, parents and teachers can provide elaborate or time-consuming reinforcements that would not be feasible each time a child made a correct response. In Jeremy's case, Mr. and Mrs. Yang first gave him pennies to exchange for the little immediate reinforcements such as juice and food that he had previously earned without the use of tokens. When the connection between pennies and food rewards was well established, they began to branch out and offer other kinds of reinforcements as well as food. For example, Jeremy could earn a car ride or time watching a video. He might be given a token every ten minutes and then be able to choose among his reinforcements after an hour. By the time he was in sixth grade,

Jeremy had learned to save his points for things he wanted during the weekend.

This chapter describes in more detail how to introduce a token system to a young child, as well as how to continue to use a token system as the learner grows up.

What Is a Token System?

In Chapter 1, we described the concept of positive reinforcement in a lot of detail. When positive reinforcement is used in teaching, your child is rewarded with an object or event immediately after a behavior. That close link between behavior and reinforcement increases the chances that the behavior will occur again in the future.

The early chapters are full of examples of how parents and teachers deliver praise and tickles and snacks and toys to increase the behaviors they are teaching. As we discussed, for some children with autism, the praise from a teacher may not function as a reinforcer (increase future behavior) initially. What the adult says does not have much meaning for the child. To address that problem, praise statements are often paired with tickling or picking up and swinging a child, or with the jellybean or popcorn the child loves. It is through this process of close association or pairing that *conditioned reinforcers* are established.

Chapter 2 describes some of the process of establishing conditioned reinforcers. Remember, a conditioned reinforcer is something that starts off as a "neutral" stimulus. This means that if that item alone were delivered to an individual after a particular behavior, it would not increase the chances of the behavior occurring again. Basically, the neutral stimulus would have no value or meaning to the learner, and would not be effective as a reinforcer or motivator.

Money is one of the most common and universal examples of conditioned reinforcement. The paper that the money is printed on and the physical coins themselves are not what makes money so valuable. The power of money lies in the fact that it can be used to purchase many things that people enjoy: new CDs, dinner at a nice restaurant, a new car, or a hot cup of coffee in the morning. Money is also a special type of conditioned reinforcer known as a *generalized* conditioned reinforcer. What this means is that the conditioned reinforcer (the money) has been paired with a large number of things, and it is associated with *many* reinforcers.

How Are Token Systems Similar to Money?

Tokens operate the same way that money does, as generalized conditioned reinforcers. Although they are initially neutral, tokens are repeatedly and systematically paired with a variety of

established reinforcers and acquire reinforcing properties. In a token system, tokens are used to reinforce desired behavior, and at a later time, the tokens can be traded in for what is known as a *back-up reinforcer*. (See Figure 5-1 on the next page for a summary of the types of reinforcement discussed in this book.)

A young child's first experience with money demonstrates how this process works. A youngster in the seat of his mother's shopping cart is given a quarter for behaving well in the grocery store. He then takes his quarter to the candy machine near the exit of the store, where he buys his back-up reinforcer and smiles with delight! A teenage boy might earn a monetary allowance for keeping his

---

Fig. 5-1 | Types of Reinforcement

Positive Reinforcement: Adding something to the environment after a response or target behavior that maintains or increases the future probability of that response under the same conditions.

Negative Reinforcement: Taking something away or out of the environment after a response or target behavior that maintains or increases the future probability of that response under the same conditions. (Examples and use of this are not discussed in this book, but you can find more information in the textbook by Cooper et al., 1987.)

Primary (Unconditioned) Reinforcer: Something that is naturally a reinforcer; it acts as a reinforcer the very first time the individual encounters it (e.g., food).

Secondary (Conditioned) Reinforcer: Something that is initially neutral, but that becomes a reinforcer over time, after being "paired" repeatedly with a primary/unconditioned reinforcer (e.g., the sign for a favorite fast food restaurant).

Generalized Conditioned Reinforcer: A specific kind of conditioned reinforcer. Something that has been paired with many different primary reinforcers (e.g., money, tokens).

Back-up Reinforcer: Something that is "purchased"; the learner exchanges tokens or money for the back-up item. A back-up reinforcer can be primary or secondary

---

room clean and participating in chores around the house. At the end of the week, he enjoys taking his savings to the music and video store to purchase a new CD.

In these examples, the tokens were coins or money. However, many types of things can be used as tokens. A token might be a sticker, a gold star, a check mark, or a smiley face that goes on a chart. A token could also be an object such as a poker chip, a bean, or a colored bead in a jar or on a string. We saw the benefits of a generalized conditioned reinforcer when points were used to motivate Jeremy Yang to complete his homework and then at the end of the week he was allowed to choose what he would like to do that weekend from many different options.

What Are the Advantages of a Token System?

Developing and using a token system has a number of advantages. For example, it may not always be feasible or practical to deliver the primary or back-up reinforcer at the moment the desired behavior happens. Ice cream may be a powerful reinforcer, but it is not always a good idea to give your child some immediately after a behavior—for example, when you want to reinforce your child's behavior of coming to the dinner table when he is called. Instead, it would be preferable to give your child a token at the moment he arrives at the table, and he can trade in the token for a bowl of ice cream after dinner. In this way, tokens can be an effective and important way to bridge a gap in time between when the behavior occurs and when the child has access to the primary reinforcer.

As we discussed in Chapter 1, it is important to provide reinforcement immediately after the behavior we want to increase. Using tokens can help us to address this concern. Tokens can be delivered quickly and easily, and are less likely to interfere with other activities. Jeremy Yang had learned to wait all week for his special weekend rewards.

Not only can token systems be useful for bridging a gap in time between the behavior and the ultimate reinforcement, but also for bridging a gap in setting as well. Imagine that you are at the playground with your child and working to increase appropriate interactions with others. Each time your child greets another child appropriately, he might earn a token. (You would give the tokens right away, so that they are linked directly to the behavior you are trying to increase.) When he returns home, he might exchange the tokens for minutes watching a favorite video or minutes playing on the trampoline. In other words, your child's most powerful reinforcers might not be available in all the settings where you wish to increase behavior. Using tokens helps you to develop and reinforce skills in those settings while taking advantage of your child's strong interest and motivation for certain activities and items.

The Yangs used tokens to bridge a gap in settings when Jeremy was younger and had trouble behaving on the school bus. They developed a program in which the bus driver gave Jeremy a token if he had not had any behavior problems during the ride home. When Jeremy got off the bus at home, he gave his father the token and was then allowed to choose from several different after-school treats.

Establishing the tokens as *generalized conditioned reinforcers* gives us yet another advantage in our teaching. Remember the concept of the establishing operation or EO discussed in Chapter 2? We described an EO as reflecting our motivation for a particular potential reinforcer at a given moment. If we are very thirsty, we have a strong EO for water, but if we just drank a full glass of water, our EO for water may be quite weak. EO's are always changing, which means that the things that will function as reinforcers are changing from moment to moment.

It is a challenge as a parent or teacher to be able to continually respond to a child's changing EO's. It is our job to create motivation and try to use rewards that will work as reinforcers, and to watch and see if our attempts are successful. Imagine that jellybeans are a powerful reinforcer for your child. However, there will be days or times of day when the jellybeans are not effective as reinforcers because his EO has changed. It may be because your child is full of (or satiated with) jellybeans. It could also be that he is not feeling well or has an upset stomach. Yet another reason could be that he has a stronger EO for something else, and that jellybeans are not as powerful in comparison at that point in time.

If, instead of using jellybeans as the only reinforcer, you use tokens, you can get around the problem of changing EO's. That is, as long as you have identified several effective reinforcers for your child, he can exchange the tokens for the one that is reinforcing to him at any given moment. For example, if you have done a preference assessment and determined that your child likes jellybeans, music, popcorn, videos, books, and tickles, you can allow him to exchange his tokens for any of those reinforcers.

The potential for broad application is an important advantage of using a token system. Tokens that are paired with a wide variety of back-up reinforcers will have more chance of being effective and will interact with your child's changing EO. Of course, it will be important to continue to assess your child's preferences, and also to systematically pair the tokens with the entire range of possible reinforcers.

Who Can Use a Token System?

You may be wondering whether a token system is appropriate for your child or learner. Token systems naturally differ in the degree of complexity and it will be important to consider this as you are introducing a token system to your child. Very young children and students who are just beginning intervention may need some specific instruction to understand the concept of the token and exchange at first. However, that does not mean that it is too early to teach them the system and that it should not be introduced. For many children, tokens will not be appropriate to bridge gaps in time or across settings in these initial stages. However, systematically using and introducing tokens will be an important foundation skill to begin building the ability to tolerate delay. Jeremy Yang was first taught to use tokens by linking pennies and food rewards very closely in time and only later became able to wait until the weekend for his back-up reinforcer.

Just as simplified token systems may be used early on, it is also possible to expand the use of token systems to address more complex behaviors and situations. Children, adolescents, and adults can benefit from individualized token systems, which will be discussed later in the chapter. The technology of token systems is widely used with individuals without disabilities in a variety of settings, such as homes, school, and even in the work place. Think of school or public library programs that award children prizes for the number of books they read over the summer break. The principles of motivation and reinforcement are central to all these applications.

Where Do You Start?

When introducing a token system to a learner for the first time, the process should be divided into four steps:

1. choosing a behavior to increase,
2. identifying back-up reinforcers,
3. choosing a token,
4. and pairing and teaching how to exchange.

We discuss these steps in detail in the sections below.

Step 1: Choosing a Behavior to Increase

Choosing a behavior to increase is something you will already have done as you read through earlier chapters in this book. The behavior should be something observable and well defined so that it will be very clear when it has occurred. For example, it might be "Touch your head," "Point to 5," or "Put the small screw in the hole."

It may also be a good idea to begin teaching about the value of tokens by starting with a behavior that your child has done successfully many times before, so that you will create many opportunities for reinforcement and practice using the tokens. The process of introducing tokens can be fun when it is applied to a well-learned behavior and with a range of highly preferred reinforcers! For example, if your child is very skilled at touching his body parts when asked (e.g., "Touch your head!"), this might be a good place to start.

Step 2: Choosing Back-up Reinforcers

Choosing back-up reinforcers is the next step. A back-up reinforcer is the object or experience for which your child is working. It

An array of back-up reinforcers for a teenaged boy.

is called a back-up reinforcer because it "backs-up" the token with a concrete reward. For example, if your child will exchange her token for a sip of juice, the juice is the back-up reinforcer. If you are not certain about how to identify potential reinforcers, you should look at Chapter 2, which reviews this topic in detail.

It will be important to offer many back-up reinforcers. Initially, you should choose something you are willing or able to give your child many times a day. For example, the following items might be used together: potato chips, pretzels, apple juice, music from a cassette player, a toy police car with siren, and a bendable cartoon character figurine. Later, back-up reinforcers can be more complex rewards, such as taking a trip to the pool or zoo.

Step 3: Choosing a Token

Many items can serve as tokens, including pennies, poker chips, pieces of colored paper, points on a scorecard, or play money. The choice of what to use for your child should be made on an individual basis.

A few things need to be considered in making this decision. The authors John Cooper, Timothy Heron, and William Heward

(1987) offer a discussion of many of these factors in their text-book, *Applied Behavior Analysis:*

1. Tokens must be relatively **portable and easy to deliver when needed.** That is why small items such as coins or chips are often used for this purpose.

2. The learner will also need **a container or place to keep the tokens** he earns until they are traded in. This might take the form of a jar, a box, a change purse, a Velcro board, or a magnetic board.

3. It is also important for tokens to be somewhat **durable,** so that they can be handled repeatedly.

4. **Safety** is another very important consideration. Often, small tokens are preferred because of their portability. However, for a very young child or a youngster who puts things in his mouth, such small tokens would not be a good choice. In those circumstances, a sticker or other symbol that could be placed on a chart might be a good choice.

5. Another point to consider is **whether the teacher or parent can maintain control over delivering the tokens.** For example, if the token is a check mark on a chart, it might be possible for a youngster to deliver his own token! Just as you control your child's access to a favorite video in order to maximize its effectiveness as a reinforcer, it is important to monitor his access to the tokens in the same way.

Sometimes, creative parents or teachers can successfully use a child's personal interest when they select tokens. For example, magnetic alphabet letters or numbers may be used, or laminated cutouts of favorite characters. Using this strategy depends on your child and the strength and nature of his particular interests. For some children, the letters of the alphabet may be very strongly associated with singing or reciting the alphabet, and this may interfere with the activity that is being taught. It is important that the tokens themselves are not so interesting that they be-

An assortment of tokens.

come distracting or interfere with the learning task at hand. Ideally, tokens selected are initially "neutral" and they gain the properties of reinforcement through pairing.

Step 4: Pairing and Teaching the Exchange Process

Teaching a child the rules of the exchange process and pairing the token with the back-up reinforcer is the last part of beginning a token system. The amount of teaching and experience a child requires with this step will vary. For many older or more advanced learners, some verbal description of the process and a brief trial period might be enough to teach the concept. Certainly, in many typical education settings, working for tokens is a very common practice. Children might be told that after their spelling test they will be given one point or one token for each word they spell correctly. At the end of the spelling lesson, the students can trade in their points for rewards of different values.

For very young children, the teaching process will need to be much more concrete. Initially, the child will need to receive one token immediately after he makes each correct response, and then immediately exchange the token for a back-up reinforcer. After several repetitions of this sequence, the child will need to earn more tokens before an exchange and learn to use a token board or container.

Figure 5-2 describes how Jeremy Yang's teacher first introduced tokens into his program. She used red poker chips as the tokens and delivered them during a program to identify body parts. Jeremy had already mastered these body parts in a previous program and she knew that he could follow these instructions quickly and easily. That allowed her to focus her effort on teaching him about the tokens. She had a variety of back-up reinforcements available to maximize the likelihood that she could capture an exciting EO that would motivate Jeremy to respond. Notice the rapid transfer of the token in the program; Jeremy is given the token and then immediately returns it to the teacher for his choice of a back-up reinforcer. The teacher gradually faded (i.e., reduced) her prompt for him to turn over the token and then required a second response before he got the token.

Keep the teaching sessions very brief initially (ten to fifteen minutes in length). At other times, you can repeat the procedure with different target behaviors that are well learned, or mixing in a few well-learned target behaviors in the same session. It will be very important to pay close attention to your child's EO. By pairing the tokens with a variety of back-up reinforcers, you can accommodate his changing EO, and ensure that the token becomes established as a generalized conditioned reinforcer.

Using the strategy described in Stage 2 of Figure 5-2, the number of tokens required for a reward can gradually be increased over a few sessions. Also, the use of a token board or container can be introduced using prompting. For example, when your child is given the first token, he can be prompted to place the token on a board or put it into a container. Depending on your child, you may help him put the token on the board or in the container using gestures (pointing to the board) or by gently guiding his hand to place the token. When it is time to make the exchange, prompt him to remove the tokens and exchange them for access to the back-up reinforcers.

Typically, children are prompted to exchange the tokens using physical guidance or visual cues such as pointing or gesturing rather than words. The goal is to help them understand the relationship between the full token board or number of tokens and the exchange. This is why the instructor does not ask the child or tell the child to make the exchange. By making the exchange process nonverbal, it is easier to fade out the physical and gestural prompts and help the child exchange independently in the future. Don't forget, one of our goals is to help individuals with autism spectrum disorders become as independent as possible, and less reliant on other people for reminders.

Fig. 5-2 | Teaching Token Exchange and Pairing

Child: Jeremy

Target Behavior: Touches body parts on request (head, nose, eyes, mouth, belly, knee, leg).

Tokens: Red poker chips.

Back-up Reinforcers: Pretzels, gummi snacks, musical book, juice with crazy straw, and colored water timer.

Procedure:
Stage 1: Pairing and 1:1 exchange
1. Arrange the back-up reinforcers at the teaching location so that Jeremy will be able to make a selection. These can be laid out on a table, the floor, in a bin, or on a large tray.
2. Present Jeremy with the instruction (e.g., "Touch your head.")
3. As soon as Jeremy performs the response, immediately give him a poker chip and praise. (If he does not give the correct response, help him complete the response and reinforce it with the praise and token. If this happens multiple times, try the training with a more consistent skill, examine the EO and back-up reinforcers available, and/or try the training at another time.)
4. Hold out your hand for the token [because we want the child to learn the sequence without relying on the instructor's directions] and immediately have Jeremy give the instructor the token using physical guidance (the instructor can prompt this or a second person can help).

Going to the Next Level: Establishing an Exchange Ratio

When you are establishing an *exchange ratio,* you are deciding how many tokens are required to "buy" the back-up reinforcers. That is, you are setting the price. In simple systems, this will be a very small number, and the back-up reinforcers will all "cost" the same. For example, 4 tokens might be exchanged for bubbles, a cracker, or playing time with a wind-up toy or xylophone. The available back-up reinforcers might change fre-

---

5. Immediately present the bin or tray or have Jeremy select an item from the array of back-up reinforcers.

6. After a minute or so with the reward, repeat the steps starting with #2. [Hopefully, your child will have experience earning reinforcers and learning that although he has to give it back, that he is able to earn another reinforcer very quickly. Often, this learning takes place while you are first using reinforcers in teaching, and before you introduce a token system. If this seems to be challenging for your child, you may need to utilize reinforcers that are slightly less powerful. Also, make sure that the task you are requiring your child to do is not too difficult, and that he will be able to earn the reward again fairly quickly.]

7. Continue the session for a few minutes, watching to make sure Jeremy is still motivated by the available back-up reinforcers. Also, watch to see if Jeremy starts handing the token to the instructor with less prompting and reaching for the back-up reinforcer after making the exchange. As soon as this occurs, move to the next stage.

Stage 2: Increasing the exchange ratio

1. Complete steps 2 and 3, above (deliver the instruction and the token reward for correct response).

2. DO NOT put your hand out to receive the token from Jeremy. Instead, deliver another instruction, and immediately reward as described in step 3 (above).

3. When Jeremy has 2 tokens, hold out your hand and prompt Jeremy to exchange BOTH tokens.

4. Allow or prompt Jeremy to select a reward from the array.

quently, according to your child's interests and the current EO's, but your child learns that she is always exchanging 4 tokens for the reward. Over longer periods of time, this number could increase to 5, 6, or possibly up to 10.

Another way to increase the number of responses that are needed to earn a back-up reinforcer is to increase the number of responses needed before each token is delivered. For example, you might give a child one instruction, praise his response, and quickly give another instruction and then provide praise and a token. Decisions about the number of responses and tokens that are needed to earn back-up reinforcers will depend on your individual child, his skills, the type of back-up reinforcement, and EO's. These variables might change from time to time as new skills are introduced, in new settings, or with different people. You will be able to get information about how well the exchange ratio is working by paying attention to your child's performance and keeping track of the number of tokens he earns and the number of opportunities he has to earn them. If he is not earning tokens on most of the opportunities, you will need to try to increase his success. Refer to the section below on troubleshooting for tips to address this problem.

Using a token board might be one way to incorporate a visual cue for your child and to make the exchange ratio more concrete. For example, if you are using smiley face tokens attached

Fig. 5-3 | Sample Token Board

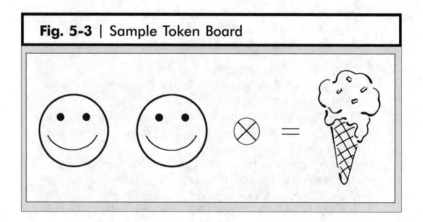

to Velcro, you might use a token board that has three patches of Velcro in a row for each token, if the exchange ratio is 3 tokens = back-up reinforcer. See an example of this in Figure 5-3. Using this design, as the child earns each token, he places it on the board and sees the number of spots remaining. When the board is full, it becomes a cue to make the token exchange.

Some parents and teachers put a picture or visual reminder of the back-up reinforcer on this type of board. For example, the board might have Velcro spots for each token, and a final spot to attach a picture of the reward the child is working toward. For some children, this visual cue may help remind them that they are earning an ice cream cone or a video. Sometimes, the teacher herself will choose the back-up reinforcer and put it on the board, or the teacher may ask the child to make the choice before he begins working. However, take care in using this type of cue. It is very important to remember the concept of EO's and how they change from moment to moment. One risk is that the EO in effect at the time a child chooses a particular back-up reinforcer may no longer be in effect when it is earned or the teacher's guess about an EO might be in error. To work effectively with a child's changing EO's, it is important to be flexible, and for some children, this strategy of a visual reminder may not be effective. In some cases, you may be able to use a word (if the child can read) or a picture representing a prize or reward to remind him that he can earn something, without specifying a particular reward.

The examples we have given so far are for an early introduction to token systems. They have to do with very specific behaviors and often are used during specific teaching sessions. This is frequently a very important and necessary way to begin using token systems. However, once the tokens have been established as generalized conditioned reinforcers, they can be used for a broad range of behaviors and in a variety of settings. Figure 5-4, on the next page, describes some other possible applications of token systems.

Fig. 5-4 | Possible Applications of a Token System

Setting	Possible Target Behavior(s)
Dinner table	Eating a bite of food; Each minute staying in seat; Using a napkin appropriately
Classroom	Raising a hand before speaking; # of flashcards answered correctly; Putting work materials away; Lining up when asked
Playground	Greeting a peer; Responding to a peer; Sharing toys/equipment appropriately
Getting ready for bed	Putting on pajama bottoms; Putting on pajama top; Putting dirty clothes in hamper; Brushing teeth
Helping with chores	Laying out place settings; Clearing each place setting; Feeding the dog; Taking out trash

Advanced Token Systems: Token Economy

As some of the examples in Figure 5-4 suggest, token systems have many possible applications for children and adolescents as they get older and develop more independence. Actually, token systems themselves are often an important key to helping children achieve greater levels of independence. Many of the parents of adolescents with autism with whom we work voice concerns about the degree of independence their teenage children show. While the youngster may be able to complete important activities of daily living (showering, dressing, brushing teeth, combing hair, or even shaving), many parents express frustration at needing to monitor and ensure that their son or daughter is completing these activities. In  some ways, this might not differ too drastically from interactions with a typically developing teenager who may not be motivated to assist with chores around the house.

One widely used strategy that may be effective for motivating a typically developing teen is giving him an allowance that is tied to the completion of a variety of tasks. Such a system is like a token system in many ways. Performing tasks results in the presentation of tokens (money), which is then exchanged (maybe at the mall) for back-up reinforcers (e.g., a new video game). One difference, however, is that the money may not be presented immediately after the behavior is performed. There is often some delay between the completion of the chore and the delivery of the allowance. Also, the fact that an adolescent may have other ways of obtaining money (e.g., through a part-time job) and other ways of getting access to a back-up reinforcer (e.g., a friend may let him play or borrow the video game) may diminish some of the power of the allowance/token system. In addition, in the allowance scenario, the adolescent is choosing his own back-up reinforcer by going to the mall to pick what he wants. This is different from a system where a parent or teacher selects an array of possible back-up reinforcers.

An advanced type of token system that is similar to the allowance example is called a *token economy*. In a token economy, there are target behaviors, tokens, and back-up reinforcers, as in the basic token systems we explained earlier. In a token economy, however, the back-up reinforcers have different values. For example, a music CD is worth 20 tokens, a cassette tape is worth 15 tokens, a pizza is worth 10 tokens, and a DVD is worth 50 tokens. In a system like this, the learner is able to "save up" the tokens over time to earn a more valuable reward, such as the DVD. The learner also has the option of using fewer tokens to "buy" a slice of pizza.

In a token economy, the parent or instructor might create a list of behaviors to be increased and assign a point value to each one. The learner can earn tokens according to the value of all the behaviors that are completed. As part of the token economy, there is also a menu describing the value or cost of each possible back-up reinforcer. The list of target behaviors and the menu of back-up reinforcers can be made using words or could be developed using pictures of the tasks and rewards. See Figure 5-5 for an example of a written list and menu.

Fig. 5-5 | Token Economy

Task	Tokens	Rewards	Cost (tokens)
Make bed	5	Watch video (30 min.)	60
Clear breakfast dishes	5	Play computer games (30 min.)	70
Hang up coat and book bag	5	Play video and games (30 min.)	70
Set table for dinner	10	Dessert/Ice Cream	55
Clear table after dinner	15	Go out to the movies on Friday	100
Take out trash	5	Go out for pizza	85
Complete homework	20	Put clothes away	5

Many of the same principles that applied to simpler systems of token exchange are relevant in the token economy. For example, it is important to monitor the effectiveness of the back-up reinforcers and to keep track of the ratio of exchange. That is, you need to ensure that the amount of work required is appropriate to the price charged for the rewards. Also, you will want to make sure that the amount of reinforcers that your child can earn are appropriate for other reasons. For instance, you would not want your child to earn more CDs than you can afford to buy him and it would not be healthy for him to earn twelve slices of pizza at one time.

The points assigned to the behaviors and the cost of each reward will need to be modified over time in order to continue to increase your child's level of independence and maintain the desired behaviors. Once your child is easily earning all of his tokens and reinforcers, you should gradually increase the cost of the back-up items over time. While it may initially cost 20 token to buy a CD, eventually your child may need to earn 30, 40, or even 50 tokens for a CD. These changes will need to be made gradually, while paying attention to your child's behavior and success. The principles involved in problem solving strategies for a token economy are the same as those for basic token systems described in the next section.

What If the Tokens Stop Working?

There could be a number of reasons why tokens may seem to "stop working." To address these problems, it will be important to remember the rules about EO's and reinforcement. When an item that usually "works" as a reinforcer does not work, it is because there is no EO in effect for that item. If popcorn has been very effective and suddenly stops working, it might be because the child is full (satiated) of popcorn. It could also be that the child is very thirsty after eating all the popcorn, and that there is a much stronger EO in effect for a drink. Making sure that the tokens have been paired with a wide range of back-up reinforcers will help to avoid this problem. It might also be important to continually reassess your child's preferences and keep adding new things to the available back-up reinforcers.

Another problem might be that the number of responses or the type of responses that are needed to earn the back-up reinforcers are too difficult for your child. There may come a point where the effort is too great, and he may give up trying to earn the reinforcers. This is similar to the concept of "response effort" that was discussed in Chapter 2.

For the process of reinforcement to occur, there must be a balance between the response requirements (the effort or amount of work required) and the reinforcement. It might be that requiring your child to make ten responses of a very hard skill is not balanced with receiving one small kernel of popcorn. To fix this problem, it is important to even out the balance. Try imagining two sides of a scale, with the number of responses on one side and the reinforcement on the other. It might be necessary to cut back and only require five responses of a particular skill before the back-up reinforcer can be earned. On the other hand, it might be that a greater amount or better quality of the back-up reinforcer might be effective. For example, you might keep the requirement at ten responses, but allow the tokens to be exchanged for a small serving of popcorn instead of a single kernel. These decisions can be made with some systematic trial and error and careful observation of your child.

In both simple token systems and token economies, it is also important to pay attention to your child's access to the back-up reinforcers. To increase the chances of having strong EO's in effect for the back-up reinforcers, make sure that he does not have the ability to get too much of the back-up reinforcers in other ways. Using popcorn as part of a token system will be less effective if your child is able to have popcorn at other times. Likewise, your child may not be motivated to earn 30 minutes of video time at the end of the day, if he is able to watch that video at other times during the day. Monitoring the general availability of these items will help increase your chances of identifying powerful EOs.

Fig. 5-6 | Questions to Ask if the Tokens Stop Working

1. Is there an EO for any of the back-up reinforcers?
2. Are there enough back-up reinforcers to choose from?
3. Is the task too difficult?
4. Are too many responses required?
5. Is the back-up reinforcer available in other ways (outside the token system)?

Fading Token Systems

You may be wondering when, if ever, it is important to move away from token systems. This is a very individual answer. In many ways, parents who offer their children allowances need to make similar types of judgment decisions. As your child becomes more and more skilled at using tokens, it is often a good idea to begin using coins or money as a reinforcer. This not only serves as a motivation system at that point, but it helps your child learn functional life skills. Your child will benefit from experiences with earning money, saving it, and using it to make purchases.

Over time, it will be important to continue modifying the system, as described above. As the skills become easier for your child, you will be able to require more for each token. This process of "upping the ante" is important and should be an ongoing process. The longer you go without requiring your child to improve his level of response and to do more to earn rewards, the harder it will be to increase the requirements over time. Ongoing, gradual change in the exchange ratios is ideal.

Likewise, you will be able to "charge" more over time for the back-up items your child is earning, particularly if you are already using money as your tokens. If not, you can begin to introduce money as tokens by pairing the actual coins or bills with the current tokens you are using. For example, if you have been giving your child 1 token for taking out the trash, you might start the transition by giving him 1 token plus 1 dollar each time he does it.

And if your child had been exchanging 15 tokens for a CD, you would now ask him for 15 dollars instead. Eventually, you can work with the prices that the items actually cost, and your child will be able to buy things at the store rather than from you.

Should you ever remove the token system completely? This is a difficult question. As adults, we are always working within a motivational system, where we are earning money, access to the things we enjoy, or some personal satisfaction or internal motivation. People with autism spectrum disorders have the same basic need for a motivational system. However, it is important to acknowledge that there will be differences. At times, it will be necessary to respect these differences, and recognize that for some learners or behaviors we may not be able to completely fade the motivational system or supports that are in place. For example, some students with autism may never be motivated to work for good grades on their report card or to please their parents or teacher and will need different kinds of reinforcers to motivate them to complete their homework. Nevertheless, the process of working toward greater independence is ongoing, and will always involve fading systems or integrating systems into the environment to whatever extent is needed to help someone be successful.

Summary

This chapter described the use of tokens as conditioned reinforcers for children and adults with autism spectrum disorders. Using tokens can be a significant advantage when it is necessary to bridge gaps between the behavior and the reinforcement across time and settings. Also, using tokens makes it unnecessary to have to identify a child's EO from moment to moment, because tokens are paired with a range of back-up reinforcers. The chapter described the use of very basic and simple token exchange systems for the early learner, as well as more advanced applications including token economies. Step-by-step guidelines for introducing tokens to your child were presented. For teachers and parents alike, tokens can be a powerful tool for increasing desirable behavior in a variety of settings.

Reference

Cooper, J. O., Heron, T. E. & Heward, W. L. (1987). *Applied Behavior Analysis.* Upper Saddle River, NJ: Merrill.

6 | Self-Management: "I Can Do It Myself"

The Hill Family

At eighteen, Kyle Hill was in many respects an accomplished young man. He had graduated from high school and was able to manage the demands of that setting academically, and socially as well—to a more modest degree in spite of his autism. Although Kyle had required considerable support from his teachers and parents, he had coped effectively with the demands of high school, earning good grades, and had seemed to benefit from the clear structure that school provided him each day. After graduation, however, the expectations in his life changed considerably. The supports that had been built into the high school program were no longer present and he was free to make many more decisions for himself without the clear expectations and guidance he had received throughout his education. This freedom proved to be a significant challenge for Kyle and for his family.

Kyle's parents contacted the Adult Resource Center for help in meeting their son's needs. They were concerned that he spent all of his time playing video games, although he had many talents and talked about finding a job and saving up so that he could move into an apartment. Because of his preoccupation with the video games, he never got around to looking at help wanted ads, preparing his resume, or seeking help from local agencies that might have been useful in finding a job. Some days he did not shave, shower, or get dressed until his parents came home from work and sent him to clean up. Mr. and Mrs. Hill were frustrated with Kyle because they knew he was capable of doing a good job as a computer technician, but he seemed unable to organize himself to look for work.

During an interview with the intake worker at the Adult Resource Center, Kyle talked at length about his wish to get a good job and live in an apartment on his own. When the intake worker asked him about the video games, he readily admitted that he spent many hours playing them. Kyle said that after his parents left for work in the morning, he would decide to play just a few games before he worked on his resume, but soon became so immersed in the games that he would forget to eat lunch. Although he was upset with himself for spending so much time playing, it was hard for him to stop.

Because of Kyle's strong motivation to stop playing the video games and get a job, the intake worker recommended that the focus of the intervention should be on teaching Kyle how to manage his own time and behavior. He was getting ready to assume a more independent life, and his parents agreed that they would support him when that was necessary but would let Kyle take the lead in changing his own behavior. The staff psychologist described the process of self-management to Kyle, and Kyle readily agreed to give the procedures a try.

Discussion

Many people with autism are motivated to change some of the behaviors that interfere with their ability to function independently. For younger children, such changes may mean being allowed more control over their choice of activities, and for adults, it may mean being able to live more independently and perhaps hold down a job. Like Kyle, they may find they do not know how to control some of the intrusive behaviors that keep them from doing other things they wish to do. Kyle Hill's seeming inability to focus on finding a job because he was drawn off track by video games is a good example. He did want a job and the paycheck that went with it, but he felt unable to stop himself from playing the video games.

For people with the motivation to do so, learning self-management methods can be a powerful way of achieving greater independence. In this chapter, we will discuss in detail some of the procedures that can be used to help a person with autism manage his or her own behavior.

What Is Self-Management?

Self-management is not just for people with autism. The field of Applied Behavior Analysis has a long history of helping individuals develop and implement systems to change their own behavior. For example, some people use self-management to decrease the number of cigarettes they smoke or the amount of food they eat. Others work on increasing the amount of exercise they do or improve their work productivity.

To be successful at these kinds of changes requires motivation. To understand why, it is useful to draw on the concept of the establishing operation (EO). If you did not read the discussion of the EO in Chapter 2, you may want to take a look now. Briefly, an EO is a description of the experiences that are currently reinforcing for an individual. If I am thirsty, I have an EO for water, and if I am lonely, I may have an EO for being with my friend. When I have an EO, I may be willing to work to gain access to the thing that will be reinforcing. Let's take the person who wants to go on a diet and lose weight. This person experiences a conflict between two EO's that are in effect—the EO for a particular food, such as chocolate cake, and the EO for being thinner, so she can wear the dress she loves. For the dieter to be successful, she needs to develop a motivation system that helps her reach her goal. When she creates that motivation system, she is doing what we call "self-management."

In technical language, self-management refers to the process of how an individual arranges her own environment to increase or decrease the occurrence of a certain behavior. For example, the dieter might decide to keep a careful record of the calories she eats and of how much exercise she gets. At the end of each day, she might graph the calories consumed and minutes of exercise, and once a week she might record her weight. The process of keeping the records by itself might be reinforcing, as she would be seeing her weight drop. To maintain her motivation, she might also set modest intermediate goals to reinforce her progress, such as buying a new, smaller size pair of slacks after she loses seven pounds, and a new bathing suit when she loses five more.

In the earlier chapters of this book, we have detailed many ways in which we, as teachers and parents, can arrange the environments of our learners in order to promote desired behavior. In Chapter 2 we discussed the importance of understanding and utilizing an individual's EO's to identify strong reinforcers to increase desired behavior. Chapter 3 was concerned with helping the young child learn to ask for what she wanted. Chapter 4 focused on choice and its important effects on behavior. Chapter 5 addressed more advanced strategies such as token systems that utilize EO's and conditioned (learned) reinforcers to build skills.

In all of these procedures, parents and teachers have a central role in identifying and maintaining the learner's motivation. For many people with autism spectrum disorders, those teacher- or parent-controlled procedures are essential steps in developing motivation to do work and conform to social demands. For older, more intellectually able learners, it is often possible to pass the process of creating motivation from the teacher or parent to them.

Why Is Self-Management Important?

Self-management is a big step beyond responding to an external structure created by someone else. Self-management can result in greatly increased independence for students with autism spectrum disorders, making this is an important and powerful technique. Over the long term, it is not ideal or even generally practical for a teacher, parent, guardian, or staff member to manage an individual's moment-to-moment motivation. Early in learning, that level of oversight is critical, but for long-term goals, we need to find ways to transfer this management to the learner herself, to whatever extent is possible. When an individual has self-management skills, she can more easily generalize (transfer) new behaviors and skills to all the settings, places, and situations where she lives and works. A motivation system that is maintained by the learner is ultimately "portable"; it goes wherever she goes.

There are other reasons why self-management strategies are important. One of these is that some behaviors are apparent to the learner herself, but not easily observed by others. For example, if someone talks to herself repetitively and nonfunctionally, she is the person who is in the best position to identify whether or not this behavior actually happened. For an observer to do this, he would need to be in very close and continuous proximity. If the person with autism can learn to monitor her own repetitive talk, she can then learn to make changes in that behavior if she is motivated to do so.

Another reason for learning self-management skills is to balance out situations in which two EO's may be competing. Remember the dieter who is faced with choosing between the immediate reinforcement of a piece of chocolate cake or the much more distant and vague reinforcement of being thinner? A behavior analyst by the name of Richard Malott (1984) referred to these two competing EO's and their corresponding reinforcement as strong and weak rules. Strong and weak refer to how much control each EO is likely to have over the behavior. For example, the chocolate cake is likely to have a stronger control over the behavior because it is concrete and immediate, whereas the concept of being thinner is much more abstract and in the future. Weak rules are likely to have less control over a behavior than are strong rules.

This same principle can be applied to an adolescent with autism or Asperger's disorder. We saw this principle at work in the experience of Kyle Hill whose vignette opened this chapter. Kyle was confronted on a daily basis with two competing EO's. On the one hand, he was very motivated to play his video games for as much time as possible. On the other hand, he wanted to get a job so that he could have an apartment and his own money one day. The video games presented a strong EO, because they were right in front of him and very concrete. His goals of having a job and getting a paycheck were much more distant and vague. A self-management system became an important part of helping to build a plan to reach the long-term goal of holding a job, even though that goal was governed by a weak rule. One of the most powerful results of a good self-management strategy is to turn weak rules into strong rules, by linking the weak rules with direct and immediate reinforcement. We will describe in detail how this might work later in the chapter.

An important element of many self-management strategies (particularly those discussed in areas of ABA outside of autism and developmental disabilities) is the individual's motivation to change or increase the specific target behavior. For example, how much does the dieter wish to change? When individuals are designing their own self-management systems, they are often extremely motivated to change a particular behavior, and are choosing to create the motivation system for themselves. Of course, this may not always be the case for learners with autism.

Our goals for our students with autism spectrum disorders are designed to help them gain access to more reinforcement from their environment and interact with others in socially appropriate ways. As parents or teachers, we may sometimes decide that behavior needs to be changed when the student is not especially motivated to make those changes. Under those conditions, we may design and implement a teaching program based on our judgment about what is important for the student. We described programs like that in the earlier pages of this book. Those teacher-determined programs are important; however, as our learners become more independent, they will be able to participate more fully in planning their own interventions and arranging their own environments to produce these changes (true self-management). Even when actual self-management is not possible, elements of these strategies can be very effective in helping someone be a part of her own interventions, reaping all of the advantages described at the beginning of this chapter.

What Is Self-Monitoring?

Becoming aware of our own behavior is often the first step toward change. One of the most valuable tools for self-management and increasing awareness is the process of self-monitoring. This refers to observing your own behavior and recording the occurrence or nonoccurrence of the specific behavior. This record keeping can take many forms. People may record their behavior in a journal or diary, or simply place check marks or tally marks on a grid or piece of paper.

Self-monitoring can be a central part of a self-management plan or any other intervention. It can be used to address behaviors that need to be increased (socializing with peers, completing activities of daily living, listening to a teacher) or behaviors that need to be decreased (engaging in stereotyped behavior, yelling out in class).

Learning to Self-Monitor Behavior

Research has shown that just the process of having someone take data on the occurrence of her own behavior can have a positive impact on the frequency of that behavior (Cooper, Heron & Heward, 1987). This positive change may be related to actually increasing the individual's awareness that she is engaging in the behavior. Common uses of self-monitoring include having a smoker document each time she smokes a cigarette or having a father who uses profanity at home record each time he does so. Sometimes the self-monitoring will result in a reduction in smoking or cursing. Other times, however, it is important to link this self-observation to other systems of rewards and consequences.

For example, a young child with autism is not often motivated to socialize with her peers in the classroom. However, she is highly motivated to play educational games on the classroom computer. The teacher may develop a self-monitoring program in which the child learns to record a mark on a small clipboard each time she approaches another child and initiates conversation or shares with her. Of course, before this can happen, the teacher has to work with the child to teach the skills needed to initiate an interaction (getting another child's attention, making eye contact, and finding something appropriate to say). The goal of the current self-monitoring program is to increase the frequency of these already mastered initiations. The system may be designed so that each interaction the child initiates is rewarded with one minute of computer time (up to five minutes) with a classmate of her choice, which she can earn at designated intervals throughout the day. The student has a chart with five check boxes on it, a reminder to talk to her friends, and a picture of the computer (Figure 6-1).

At the beginning of this intervention, the teacher will have to help the child learn to record her own data accurately. The teacher might help the child fill out the grid initially, and then watch and give the child feedback about the accuracy of her data after each opportunity, whether or not she recorded it correctly. Over time, the teacher may be able to fade his or her help completely, and only observe the child's data periodically.

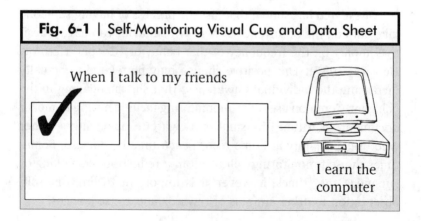

Fig. 6-1 | Self-Monitoring Visual Cue and Data Sheet

When I talk to my friends

I earn the computer

The self-monitoring strategy described above helps to successfully increase the child's awareness of her own behavior, enhances her independence, and also allows the teacher to engage in other activities while still monitoring and intervening to address this student's behavior.

Sometimes, a videotape can be used to help a student learn to identify and record her own behavior. For instance, a young girl who engages in periodic stereotyped behavior during group learning activities, such as waving her hands or fingers, may need to learn how to identify this behavior when it occurs. (For an example, see the sample data sheet in Figure 6-2.) However, it may be very disruptive to try to teach her this skill while she is participating in a group. To begin teaching this concept of self-observation and recording, a teacher may videotape the student during the group lesson, while she engages in the stereotyped behavior. Later, the teacher might watch the video together with the child and help her identify instances of the behavior. With practice, the child can learn to collect data regarding the frequency of the behavior from the videotapes, and the teacher can monitor her accuracy. The child may be given bonus reinforcement for accurate data, in addition to reinforcement for decreasing levels of the target behavior.

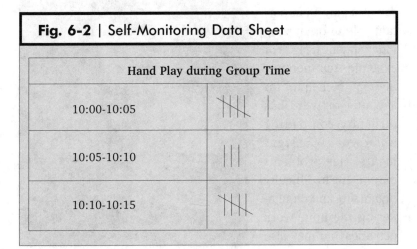

Fig. 6-2 | Self-Monitoring Data Sheet

Hand Play during Group Time	
10:00-10:05	卌 |
10:05-10:10	|||
10:10-10:15	卌

After this recording skill is well learned, and the student can identify the behavior and accurately record it, the teacher may begin to transfer the self-monitoring process to the actual setting where the behavior is happening. Using the same type of chart or data sheet, the teacher may begin by tapping the student on the shoulder and silently gesturing to the data sheet, indicating that she should record an occurrence of the behavior. Again, the teacher may include some type of reinforcement for the child if she records data accurately.

Note that even if a child is not motivated to change/stop a behavior, she may be motivated to earn a reinforcer. In this situation, our work often involves trying to identify reinforcers that will "compete" with the behavior. For example, permission to watch a video might be a stronger reinforcer for a child than waving her hands in front of her face. In these cases, the child is not participating in true self-management, as she is not identifying behaviors to change or expressing a desire to change them. However, she can still benefit from self-monitoring, a component of self-management.

Using Self-Monitoring to Increase Independence

Self-monitoring can also play an important role in organizing independent tasks. For example, self-monitoring may be helpful for a youngster who has difficulty completing homework assignments. Her problems may be due to difficulty organizing and remembering the homework activities, but may also

be due to competing EO's. For example, the child may prefer to watch television or play with her action figure toys rather than complete the two worksheets that are required for homework. Using a "to do" list or a schedule may help to focus her and organize the activities and the rewards. She can be taught to list each item that needs to be completed and designate the reward that will be available after the items are completed. For some learners, it is very helpful to be able to check off each activity as it is completed.

Creating checklists may also be a useful strategy for self-evaluation of performance. This may become increasingly relevant as an adolescent is training for a vocational activity. For example, we know a young man who was very skilled and independent at completing a sequence of cleaning activities. After cleaning a room, he learned to evaluate his performance by reviewing a checklist. See Figure 6-3 for examples of items that might be included in his list.

After completing the quality control checklist appropriately, this young man was able to take a snack and magazine break, which was a very preferred activity. Using this self-monitoring strategy, he not only continued to complete the activities independently, but he also increased the quality of his work and could generate social reinforcement from his job coach by reviewing the list with her. He enjoyed praise, and reviewing the list created a natural opportunity for him to receive attention and praise.

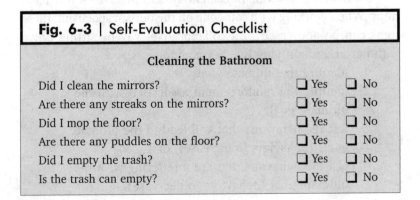

Fig. 6-3 | Self-Evaluation Checklist

Cleaning the Bathroom		
Did I clean the mirrors?	❑ Yes	❑ No
Are there any streaks on the mirrors?	❑ Yes	❑ No
Did I mop the floor?	❑ Yes	❑ No
Are there any puddles on the floor?	❑ Yes	❑ No
Did I empty the trash?	❑ Yes	❑ No
Is the trash can empty?	❑ Yes	❑ No

Putting It All together: Developing a Self-Management System

Before helping your child or student on the autism spectrum develop a self-management system, you should be reasonably certain she is ready for one. Someone is likely to be a good candidate for a self-management system if:

1. She has successfully implemented a self-monitoring system that was designed by someone else, such as a teacher or parent.

2. She has shown the ability to select and deliver her own reinforcement. For example, she is able to select activities and reinforcers for her own activity schedule, as described in Chapter 4, and independently follow it. Or, she is able to use a token system by selecting a reward and exchanging tokens, as described in Chapter 5.

It is also very helpful for the learner to have an understanding of basic math skills, so that she can tell from her data whether her behavior is increasing or decreasing.

Key Components of a Self-Management Plan

Developing a self-management system involves a few basic steps. When working with someone on the autism spectrum, these steps can be addressed in a collaborative way by sitting down with her and identifying five key components:

1. Identify the ultimate goal.

2. Identify the reinforcement associated with the ultimate goal.

3. List the behaviors that will lead to the ultimate goals (behaviors to increase), or

4. List the behaviors that are interfering with the ultimate goal (behaviors to decrease).

5. Identify potential reinforcement for increasing or decreasing the target behaviors(s).

First, let's use these components to consider how the dieter might apply them. The ultimate goal is the long-term objective the individual would like to achieve. For example, in the case of the person on a diet, this might be to lose 20 pounds and be able to walk 3 miles in 45 minutes. The reinforcement associated with the ultimate goal refers to the long-term reinforcements such as better health, greater endurance, a stronger body, slimmer appearance, and so forth that are appealing to the dieter. The behaviors that will lead to the ultimate goal include such things as taking a walk each day, eating smaller portions, changing the kinds of food consumed, etc. The behaviors that are interfering with the ultimate goal might include the urge to eat a piece of pizza or to succumb to the temptation of that chocolate cake. Finally, the dieter's reinforcers for decreasing eating and increasing exercise might include seeing progress on her graphs of weight and exercise, buying a new item of clothing at specific points in weight loss, or telling other people about her progress.

Developing a self-management system for someone with an autism spectrum disorder follows a similar pattern, although it may take more effort in the beginning to help the individual understand the plan. Through conversation with the learner, you can define all of the elements and together design a specific plan that she can use to manage her behavior. Let's look at how this worked for Kyle when he participated in creating a self-management plan to get a job. Note that these behaviors, while appropriate for Kyle, might not be appropriate for your own learner.

1. **The ultimate goal.** Kyle would like to live independently one day in an apartment, possibly with roommates. He would like to have a job that generates a modest income, in addition to the support he receives from his parents.

2. **The reinforcement associated with the ultimate goal.** Kyle said that he would enjoy the personal freedom of living on his own. The money he earns would allow him to contribute significantly to his basic expenses and also give him the ability to buy things for himself such as videos, CDs, and video games.

3. **The behaviors that will lead to the ultimate goals (behaviors to increase).** Good hygiene will be a very important component to increasing Kyle's employment possibilities. He also needs to engage in a sequence of job search behaviors. Learning to keep to an independent hygiene routine, sitting down at the computer to write his resume, checking the paper for help wanted ads, visiting the local job support program for help in finding a job are prerequisites to functional employment.

4. **The behaviors that are interfering with the ultimate goal (behaviors to decrease).** Kyle is currently watching videos and playing video games at a frequency that interferes with his hygiene activities and job search.

5. **Potential reinforcement for increasing or decreasing the target behavior(s).** Make Kyle's access to the videos and games depend on his successful completion of the specified activities. Also structure his engagement in these activities (by restricting his access to the VCR and computer and by using a timer) to help him adhere to the plan.

With Kyle's input, the beginnings of a self-management plan were developed. Kyle was able to articulate his ultimate goal and recognize the steps that would help lead to this goal. However, simply identifying these goals, behaviors, and reinforcement was not sufficient on its own. It was important to establish that Kyle was capable of doing these activities independently. That is, it was necessary to confirm that the problem was truly due to difficulties with motivation and not to a lack of skills. It was also important to explore the response effort required to engage in the target behavior. Is it difficult for Kyle to take care of his hy-

giene? Organize his resume? Does he know how to read the help wanted ads? With Kyle, we determined that helping him place his grooming materials into organized drawers and baskets would be a significant help. We also taught him how to read the help wanted ads and coached him in how to call the local job agency. Providing him with a written reminder of the steps involved (and the immediate and ultimate rewards) was helpful.

Kyle also admitted that he was not sure that he would be able to stick to the rules that were developed for his reinforcement. For example, he might be tempted to watch a video even though he had not completed the steps he agreed upon. He also indicated that he might have difficulty stopping the video games after the set time limit, although he had agreed upon the time limit ahead of time. To assist in these aspects of the self-management plan, Kyle agreed to initially allow his mother to keep the video games and videos, and that he would be able to get them from her when she came home from work on her lunch hour or in the evening after work, whenever he earned them. He also agreed to set and use a timer in order to structure his time with the games or videos. Using the timer, he was able to stop the game and save his progress or stop the video so he could resume at the same place the next time he earned the video. These strategies helped him stick to the guidelines he helped to create.

For Kyle, watching videos and playing video games was sufficiently reinforcing to motivate him to follow his self-management plan. If these activities had not been reinforcing enough, his plan could have included additional reinforcement, such as 50 cents in a jar for each day he completed his goals. This kind of reinforcement would also help an individual to earn and save money to purchase additional and novel reinforcement over time.

The example with Kyle illustrates the basic steps involved in developing and implementing a self-management system. The level of involvement and collaboration will vary from individual to individual and depend on the specific behaviors of interest. However, the advantages of allowing people with autism spectrum disorders to participate in their own intervention and increasing independence are clear.

As we discussed earlier in the chapter, self-management may not be ideal for everyone. However, it is an important goal to consider and work toward, even when an individual is not yet able to articulate her goal and desired reinforcement. She may still benefit from self-monitoring or the use of checklists, and, over time, may be able to contribute more and more to the development of her own plan. A learner's preferences should always be considered when selecting behaviors to change and procedures to use.

What If the System Stops Working?

What if you have successfully implemented a self-management procedure, and, after some period of success, the plan stops working? Perhaps the individual has become less accurate in her data collection and monitoring, or become less interested in the rewards. These obstacles are related to the fundamental principles we have reviewed throughout the book. As always, it is critical to examine the EO. Is the EO strong enough? Are the rewards varied enough?

It is also important to assess the effort that is involved, and how this relates to the reward. Here, there are two types of effort to consider. First, the effort needed to complete the desired behavior (e.g., talk to a peer, complete the hygiene activities) is one consideration. For example, if we had not helped Kyle to organize all the necessary hygiene steps, then the response effort may have been too great for him to be able to be successful and receive reinforcement.

Second, it is also important to consider the effort that is required to record the data. This factor sometimes accounts for a decrease in the accuracy of the self-monitoring data. In Kyle's situation, it was important to discuss how he was going to collect the data about his progress each day. For example, asking Kyle to write down each hygiene step that he completed in a notebook in his room was not practical. It was much easier for him to record a checkmark on a list that was posted in the bathroom.

Frequently, in our work with individuals on the autism spectrum, we have found that they enjoy the process of record-keeping. We have not often encountered questions regarding why data is needed. In many cases, it may be sufficient to explain that the data are needed in order to know whether the reinforcement was earned. Without some sort of record, there would be no way to know if the required tasks were completed or if the behavior occurred at the appropriate level.

It is crucial to balance the effort involved in completing the behavior and recording the data with the strength and power of the EO for the reinforcement. In other words, the reward has to be rewarding enough for the amount of work you expect the individual to do. If the learner's EO for the potential reinforcers is relatively weak, and the requirements of the tasks and the data collection are too difficult, it is not likely that the system will be effective.

It is also important to recognize the need for a flexible system that changes with the individual's needs and progress. Even well-developed plans that we create for ourselves can encounter unforeseen obstacles. As adults, many of us can think of plans we developed to change our own behavior that were less than completely successful. Circumstances change over time, as do priorities and motivation. These factors are no different for people with autism spectrum disorders. Therefore, a vital step to take if a self-management plan stops working is to talk with your child or student to see if anything has changed since the initial plan was created. You might bring up and discuss the five key questions you posed when first developing the plan.

Keeping in mind that this is a natural process may help us to revise and develop new plans, rather than incorrectly assuming that a given individual cannot effectively use self-management.

Summary

As described in this chapter, true self-management occurs when an individual actively designs and implements her own intervention. Although this may not be possible for everyone with autism, the chapter describes ways of introducing concepts involved in self-management. For instance, with self-monitoring, a person can learn to observe and record her own behavior, an important first step in self-management.

As your child or student masters self-management strategies, you may be able to transfer the process of establishing and maintaining her motivation from a parent or teacher to the individual herself. Using self-management strategies might enable her to decide for herself what goals she would like to achieve and how she will achieve them. For example, she might choose to decrease interfering behaviors, increase social skills, improve academic performance, and learn new adaptive skills needed for daily living. Ultimately, self-management skills may be the key to help her achieve the greatest level of independence possible across all areas of life.

References

Malott, R. W. (1984). In search of human perfectibility: A behavioral approach to higher education. In W. L. Heward, T. E. Heron, D. S. Hill & J. Trap-Porter (Eds.), *Focus on Behavior Analysis in Education* (pp. 218-245). Columbus, OH: Charles E. Merrill.

Cooper, J. O., Heron, T. E., & Heward, W. L. (1987). *Applied Behavior Analysis.* Upper Saddle River, NJ: Prentice Hall.

INDEX

Activities of daily living. *See* Independence

Activity schedules, 82-84

Activity Schedules for Children with Autism, 82

Adults with ASD. *See* Independence; Work

Allowance, 113

Applied Behavior Analysis, 6-7, 123

Applied Behavior Analysis (book), 6, 17, 105

Arrays
of clothing, 77
of reinforcers, 38

Associations. *See* Pairing

Back-up reinforcers. *See* Reinforcers, back-up

Behavior Modification (book), 6, 17

Behavioral definition, 57

Behaviors. *See also* Compliance, teaching
as communication, 48
awareness of, 127
decreasing, 127, 132
escape or avoidance, 5
increasing, 103, 127, 132
making choices and, 87-90
rigid, 81
self-injurious, 88
self-management of, 122-27
self-monitoring, 127-31
seriously maladaptive, 6
stereotyped, 5, 12, 127, 129
tantrums, 70, 88, 89, 90

Bondy, Andy, 52

Bribery, 9-10

Case studies
Barton family, 1-2
Brown family, 19-20
Dunn family, 47-48
Hill family, 121-22
Ramirez family, 73-74
Yang family, 95-96

Checklists, self-evaluation, 131. *See also* Schedules

Children with ASD
building rapport with, 56
identifying preferences of, 39-41
observing preferences of, 28-33

Choices, making
activity schedules and, 83-87
at school, 91-92

at work, 88-90
behavior management and,
   87-90
importance of, 74-75
teaching, 75-80
troubleshooting problems
   with, 80-81
Clothing, choosing, 77-80
Communication problems.
   See also Sign language;
   PECS
Mand training for, 51-52
receptive language difficul-
   ties, 71
Compliance, teaching, 53-56
Comprehension problems, 71
Consequences, 57
Cooper, John, 104
Cues. *See* Prompts
Data collection, 57, 59-60,
   129, 137
DeLeon, Iser, 38
DeLeon and Iwata procedure,
   38-39
Delmolino, Lara, 148
Deprivation, 22, 27
Description of program, 57
Dieting, 124, 133
Discriminative stimulus, 50, 57
Douglass Developmental
   Disabilities Center, 57, 148
Dressing, 77-80
EO. *See* Establishing operation
Errorless learning, 62-63
Establishing operation
   conflicts with, 123, 125, 131

evocative effect, 25-26
importance of, 25
reinforcer establishing
   effect, 25
responding to changes in,
   101-102, 107, 111, 115
Exchange ratio, 109-11
Fading. *See* Prompts, fading
Fisher, Wayne, 36
Fisher method, 36-38
Food reinforcers, 15
Frost, Lori, 52
Functional assessment, 89
*Functional Assessment and
   Program Development for
   Problem Behavior,* 6
Generalization, 63, 89, 125
Harris, Sandra L., 148
Heron, Timothy, 104
Heward, William, 104
Homework, 130-31
Imitation, 5
Independence
   using schedules to increase,
      84-87
   using self-management to
      increase, 124-25
   using self-monitoring to
      increase, 130-31
   using token economies to
      increase, 112-15
Interests. *See* Preferences
Intraverbals, 49
Iwata, Brian, 38
Krantz, Patricia, 82

Language problems. *See*
    Communication problems
Language, receptive, 71
Manding
    definition of, 49-50
    how to teach, 53-69
    troubleshooting problems
        with, 70-71
    when to teach, 52—53
    who can benefit from, 51-52
Making a Difference, 7, 17
Malott, Richard, 125
Maurice, Catherine, 7
McClannahan, Lynn, 82
Mental retardation, 4, 51
Michael, Jack, 24
Money, 97-98, 113, 117
Motivation. *See also* Estab-
    lishing operation; Prefer-
    ences children with ASDs
    and, 3, 4
    definition of, 20-21
    first step in, 28
    importance of, for learning, 4
    role of reinforcement in,
        21-24
    self-management and, 122,
        123, 124, 126
    typically developing children
        and, 3-4
Motivational Operation. *See*
    Establishing Operation
Natural Environment Training
    (NET), 50
Nonverbal children. *See*
    Communication problems

O'Neill, R.E., 89
Pace, Gary, 34
Pace method, 34-36
Pairing, 13, 42, 97, 99
Parents
    as partners in play, 54
    building rapport, 56
    role in motivating typically
        developing children, 4
Partington, James, 50, 53, 54,
    55, 71
PECS, 52, 56
Photographic activity sched-
    ules. *See* Activity schedules
A Picture's Worth, 52
Play. *See also* Socialization
    skills; Toys
    mand training and, 54-55
Praise
    as incentive for children
        with ASDs, 4, 24, 43, 118
    pairing with tangible
        rewards, 12-13
Preferences
    Fisher method of assessing,
        36-38
    identifying your own
        child's, 39-41
    observing child's, 28-33
    Pace method of assessing,
        34-36
Pretending
    difficulties in, 6
Prompts
    fading, 62, 66, 68
    nonverbal, 108

time delay of, 58-61
Reaching Out, Joining In, 6, 17
Receptive language, 71
Record keeping. *See* Data
   collection
Reinforcement
   negative, 10, 99
   points to remember
      about,11
   positive, 8-10, 97, 99
Reinforcers. *See also* Establishing Operation; Token
   systems
age appropriate, 42
array of, 38
back-up, 98, 99, 100, 103-
   104, 109, 110
bribery and, 9-10
conditioned, 97-98, 99
controlling access to, 55,
   105, 116
ease of obtaining, 54, 116,
   137
examples of, 13-15, 114,
   128, 136
generalized conditioned,
   98, 99, 111
importance of identifying
   variety of, 2, 12
ineffective, 39, 115
introducing new, 35, 41-44
long-term, 133
observing which ones are of
   interest, 28-33
pairing, 13, 42, 97, 99
people as, 42-43

primary, 99, 100
rules for giving, 11-13, 105
secondary, 99
social, 12, 43
timing of, 100
unconditioned, 99
using for motivation, 21-24
visual reminders of, 111
Requests. *See* Manding
Response effort, 26, 116
Rewards. *See* Reinforcers
Right from the Start, 7, 17
Rigidity, 81
Rules, strong or weak, 125,
   126
S^D, 50, 57
Satiation, 22, 27
Schedules
   benefits of choosing own, 81
   for homework, 131
   photographic activity, 81-84
   teaching child to make,
      84-87
   written, 83-84
School
   choice making at, 91-92
   homework, 130-31
   self-management at, 128
Self-care skills. *See*
      Independence
Self-management
   definition of, 122-24
   importance of, 124-27
   key components of, 132-36
   readiness for, 132
   self-monitoring and, 127-31

troubleshooting, 136-38
Self-stimulatory behavior. *See*
    Behavior, self-stimulatory
Sensory problems, 80
Sign language, 51-52, 56
Skinner, B.F., 49
Socialization skills, 128. *See*
    also Play
Speech difficulties. *See also*
    Communication problems
    manding and, 51-53
Stereotyped behavior. *See*
    Behavior, stereotyped
Sundberg, Mark, 50, 53, 54,
    55, 71
Tacts, 49
Tantrums, 70, 89, 90. *See also*
    Behaviors
Target behavior, 57
Teaching Language to Children
    with Autism or Other
    Developmental Disabilities,
    50
Teaching programs, elements
    of, 57
Timer, 135-36
Token systems
    addressing changes in EO
        with, 101-102, 107, 111,
        115
    advantages of, 100-102
    exchange ratio and, 109-11
    fading, 117-18
    introducing use of, 103-108
    possible applications of, 112
    purpose of, 98-100

token economies and, 112-15
tokens used with, 99,
    104-106
troubleshooting, 115-17
who can use, 102-103
Toys, 41
    motivating, 30
Verbal behavior, 50
Videotapes, 129
Work, 89, 126, 131, 133, 134

About the Author

Sandra L. Harris, Ph.D., is a Board of Governors Distinguished Service Professor at the Graduate School of Applied and Professional Psychology and the Department of Psychology at Rutgers, The State University of New Jersey. She is the Founder and Executive Director of the Division of Research and Training at the Douglass Developmental Disabilities Center at Rutgers, which serves people with autism from preschool through adulthood.

Lara Delmolino, Ph.D., is a Research Assistant Professor at the Graduate School of Applied and Professional Psychology at Rutgers, and Assistant Director for Research at the Douglass Developmental Disabilities Center. She is also a Board Certified Behavior Analyst.